Since leaving her American homeland in 2003, Belén Fernández had been an inveterate traveler. Ceaselessly wandering the world, the only constant in her itinerary was a conviction never to return to the country of her childhood. Then the COVID-19 lockdown happened, and Fernández found herself stranded in a small village on the Pacific coast of Mexico.

This charming, wryly humorous account of nine months stuck in one place nevertheless roams freely: over reflections on previous excursions to the wilder regions of North Africa, Asia, and Eastern Europe; over her newfound friendship with Javier, the mezcal-drinking, chain-smoking near-septuagenarian she encounters in his plastic chair on Mexico's only clothing-optional beach; over her protracted struggle to obtain a life-saving supply of yerba mate; and over, literally, the rope of a COVID-19 checkpoint, set up directly outside her front door and manned by armed guards who require her to don a mask every time she returns hom

CHECKPOINT ZIPOLITE

CHECKPOINT ZIPOLITE
QUARANTINE IN A SMALL PLACE

BELÉN FERNÁNDEZ

OR Books
New York · London

Published by OR Books, New York and London
Visit our website at www.orbooks.com

Some of the material in this book is adapted from the essay "Coronastalgia" (Belén Fernández, *Evergreen Review*, November 2020), with permission from the publisher.

All rights information: rights@orbooks.com

First printing 2021

Library of Congress Cataloging-in-Publication Data: A catalog record for this book is available from the Library of Congress.
British Library Cataloging in Publication Data: A catalog record for this book is available from the British Library.

Typeset by Lapiz Digital.

paperback ISBN 978-1-68219-306-8 • ebook ISBN 978-1-68219-261-0

For Mama

Nothing happens until something moves.

—Albert Einstein

On the back page of a green-and-blue notebook I bought some years ago at a supermarket in Tunis is scribbled a was-to-have-been travel itinerary for 2020. It's a mess of airport codes, bus and ferry times, visa reminders, and marks indicating the locations—Beirut and Barcelona among them—that offer straightforward options for stockpiling Argentine yerba mate, a beverage critical to my existence. The final date that appears on the itinerary—in handwriting that over the years has become decreasingly legible even to me, presumably a form of overcompensation for the neurotically meticulous script I maintained throughout childhood—is October 12, which is as far as I had gotten during my last bout of travel planning in San Salvador, where I had arrived in December of 2019 for a three-month stay.

The comparatively lengthy Salvadoran sojourn (requiring seven kilos of Barcelona-acquired yerba mate crammed into my suitcase) was itself a deviation from a modus operandi of accelerated international movement that had commenced with my abandonment of the United States after graduating college in New York in 2003. In the months preceding El Salvador, I had gone from Turkey to Puglia in the south of Italy to Croatia-Bosnia-Croatia-Bosnia-Croatia-Bosnia to Turkey-Albania-Corfu-Spain-Tbilisi-Yerevan-Spain. The manic itinerancy was meant to resume upon my departure from the diminutive Central American nation where neocon extraordinaire and Iran-Contra convict Elliott Abrams had once praised the Reagan administration's record as one of "fabulous achievement." Fabulousness had included the December 11, 1981 massacre of up to twelve hundred people in the Salvadoran village of El Mozote by the U.S.-trained and -funded Atlacatl Battalion. On December 12, Abrams had taken up a post as Reagan's assistant secretary of state for human rights and humanitarian affairs [*sic*], and had set about denying that any such massacre had ever transpired. In all, the Salvadoran civil war of 1980–92 killed upwards of seventy-five thousand people, with the vast majority of lethal violence committed by the U.S.-backed right-wing military and allied paramilitary outfits and death squads.

When I first committed to three full months in El Salvador, the feeling that I was signing up for the equivalent of marriage and reproduction was assuaged only by the awareness that, come March 2020, I'd be dashing around Mexico before flying to Istanbul and resuming freneticism in that hemisphere. Little did I know that the scribbled itinerary would never come to fruition, and that I'd only get as far as the coastal village of Zipolite in the Mexican state of Oaxaca, where March 13–25 would turn into March 13 until further notice.

In San Salvador I had rented a studio apartment across from the Estadio Cuscatlán, where on not-too-hungover mornings I jogged in the parking lot, which was perennially coated in a layer of glass shards that had once formed Pilsener, Suprema, and Regia beer bottles.

The soccer stadium boasted a bevy of humbly equipped security guards, fixtures of the Salvadoran landscape, who took turns patrolling the grounds on a decrepit bicycle. Slightly spiffier guards were on hand at the Súper Selectos supermarket down the street, which was my other principal pedestrian destination in a metropolis thoroughly inconducive to ambulatory movement. Obstacles to motion would expand in the final stretch of my stay, when I was bitten in the leg by a dog and reduced to sitting by my window staring at a palm tree and the volcano in the distance, in between hopping to the bathroom and fridge.

Metropolitan navigation was decidedly more complicated for Salvadorans themselves, however, whose lives, unlike mine, were governed by ubiquitous invisible borders delineating territory controlled by rival gangs. This meant that an act as simple as crossing the street could literally constitute a death sentence. There were also, of course, socioeconomic barriers to contend with, as in the case of gated communities with watchtowers, or malls and other establishments where the clean and cheery flow of capital must never be impeded by a surplus of representatives of the unsightly underclasses.

Then there was the issue of the effective criminalization of tattoos—or, more generally, youth—by Salvadoran law enforcement personnel, who delighted in extrajudicial activity and were known for costarring in contemporary news headlines such as this one from CNN: "US-funded police linked to illegal executions in El Salvador." New opportunities for creative trigger-happiness would arise in accordance with the coronavirus lockdown imposed by Salvadoran president Nayib Bukele shortly following my exit from the country. In one episode, as a *Bloomberg* opinion article reported, "security forces mistook a young woman who'd gone shopping for a Mother's Day present for a criminal gang member and shot her dead."

One component of Bukele's worldview was the notion that United States president Donald Trump "is very nice and cool, and I'm nice and cool, too . . . we both use Twitter a lot, so, you know, we'll get along." A month into the lockdown, he would take to said social media platform to authorize the Salvadoran army and police to employ lethal force against gang members (read: Mother's Day shoppers). The tweet-decree specified that such force was justified in self-defense "or in defense of the lives of Salvadorans." Another presidential tweet from around the same time specified that "the rumors of my kidnapping by aliens are completely unfounded." And if any doubt remained as to Bukele's soundness of mind or commitment to saving Salvadoran lives, he also began jampacking unsanitary "containment centers" with alleged violators of the quarantine, suspected carriers of COVID-19, and Salvadorans returning from abroad—with predictable results.

Bukele's cool counterpart to the north meanwhile forged ahead with deportations, doing his own part for virus propagation. Trump's coolness fortunately hadn't been jeopardized by his reference to El Salvador as a "shithole" country, nor had the shithole designation jeopardized El Salvador's eligibility, in Trump's eyes, to serve as a so-called "safe third country," i.e., a dumping ground for migrants seeking asylum in the United States. Never mind that many asylum seekers hailed from El Salvador in the first place precisely because it was the opposite of safe—a state of affairs the U.S. has had pretty much everything to do with. The gangs that are forever blamed for El Salvador's appalling levels of violence and invoked by the Salvadoran government as carte blanche for murder are a product of none other than a previous deportation era: at the end of the Salvadoran civil war, the U.S. undertook a mass expulsion of members of gangs that had formed around Los Angeles as a means of communal defense for Salvadorans fleeing the overwhelmingly U.S.-backed terror in their country. Fabulous all around.

For many Salvadorans, naturally, the postwar panorama of physical and economic brutality did not provide a compelling reason to stay put, although the northward journey has become increasingly perilous thanks to sociopathic refinements to U.S. border-fortification schemes. For me, on the other hand, El Salvador did technically qualify as a safe third country of sorts, given that my own chief migratory preoccupation was simply avoiding the U.S. at all costs, as I had determined the homeland to be irreparably creepy and hazardous to my health (a shithole, if you will). And yet, thanks to my passport privilege, I was also able to extricate myself from the place as desired and make my way to Mexico without having to risk kidnapping, rape, disappearance, or any of the other potential outcomes of unprivileged migration.

And so it was that on March 9 I headed to the airport named for beloved Salvadoran Archbishop Óscar Romero, whose critiques of right-wing atrocities and the injustices of capitalism had gotten him assassinated almost exactly four decades before. I flew to Mexico City, where I spent the night hopping around the terminal—still on account of the dog bite—after an attempt to sleep on the floor was thwarted by a security guard's insistence that I remain upright at all times. As per my standard airport behavior, I alternated between adrenaline rushes induced by the departure screens—and all of the possibilities contained therein—and a feeling of immense pressure to simultaneously be in all of those places. On top of this, too, was my ever-present curiosity re: how much more productive and/or fulfilling my life would be if I didn't spend so much time imagining myself in places other than the one I was in.

Indeed, I had come to view my condition as a kind of acute attention deficit disorder in the form of itinerancy. I also suspected that there was something very inherently American about the aspirations to omnipresence, and the idea that I really could have it all. But even the obscene luxury of being able to go pretty much wherever I pleased—at least as long as my freelancing income covered the bills, which were inevitably far lower outside the U.S. no matter how much I darted about—came with its own grass-is-always-greener element. At times, faced with seemingly infinite travel options, I found myself experiencing wistfulness for a certain tiny grocery store I patronized in Havana in 2006, where the stack of shelves offered precisely one brand of canned pork product and nothing else. Obviously, the greener-grass perspective worked in other directions, as well—as with my father's relatives in eastern Cuba, whose list of grievances against Fidel Castro included that bathroom renovations had been stalled since 1962.

From Mexico City, my connecting flight was to Oaxaca City, where I spent three nights in a room that in real life resembled a prison cell rather more than it had in the pictures. The room belonged to a house atop a hill, a less than ideal location to reach by hopping, but a nearby overlook offered a spectacular view of the sunrise and other people's laundry. It was here that the coronavirus first entered my consciousness as something more than #Wuhan, which had been a perpetual trending topic on Twitter in El Salvador, alongside more local themes like Nayib Bukele, earthquakes, and Jesus Christ. On March 11, the World Health Organization declared COVID-19 a pandemic and Trump announced his European travel ban, one of various ostensible counter-COVID measures that would additionally involve enlisting the services of his prized son-in-law in a secretive task force, prompting even *The New York Times* to run the headline "Jared Kushner Is Going to Get Us All Killed" (the wording was subsequently sanitized). Also on March 11, I got an email from my Italian musician friend Gianluca, who held the distinction of being the first person I met when I left the U.S. in 2003. He informed me that he and his mother, Adriana, were under de facto house arrest in Puglia—a concept I found just as inconceivable some days later when my parents reported the same thing from their apartment in Barcelona. My mom soon began sending me fast-motion videos of my dad marching in circles around the kitchen table, down the short hallway to the bedroom and back—clocking, according to his Fitbit, 130 kilometers in the first eighteen days of lockdown.

Adriana herself was like a deputy mom to me, and since 2004 I had descended upon her humble beach house nearly every summer for a month of village gossip, mosquitoes, and binging on cheese in the middle of the night. As Gianluca resided outside of Napoli and only rarely made it to Puglia for a visit, the co-quarantine was a relative stroke of luck for Adriana, who, forever accusing her son of willful malnutrition, was able to exploit the pandemic to conduct authoritarian feeding sessions. When I received Gianluca's email, my brain had not yet fully acclimated to the notion that coronavirus was A Thing, and I responded with a snotty rant about how if Italians really cared about death why didn't they care about all the refugees drowning off their coast. At any rate, I reasoned, whatever was going on with that part of the world would surely be sorted by July, when I was scheduled to arrive to Puglia by ferry from Albania.

Zipolite, so it's said, means *la playa de la muerte*—the beach of death—although I did not find this out until more than two months into my stay in the village when a wave almost killed me. Zipolite had been selected as a destination based on a quick Google search for "beaches Oaxaca" during the particularly energetic San Salvador hangover that had produced a good part of the back-of-notebook itinerary. These periodic travel-planning frenzies, while supplying the requisite sense of chaos and adventure, also allowed me a certain feeling of control over the universe. Granted, things like eighty-five-hour flights to Sri Lanka via absurd combinations of non-U.S. airports always sounded more exciting during the planning phase. Zipolite had also been chosen as a suitable point for international rendezvous with Marwan, a Lebanese-Palestinian friend whose own travels were severely hindered by his Lebanese passport but who was able to obtain a Mexican visa without jumping through dehumanizing hoops.

The bus ride from Oaxaca City entailed seven hours of mountain curves and speedbumps taken at high speed—something I should have known seeing as I had hitchhiked the very same route with my Polish friend and former travel companion Amelia in 2005. That trip had taken place primarily in the back of a pickup truck, which is perhaps why I had blocked the details from memory. This time around, I at least had a seat in which to lurch violently while the Austrian in the next row pathologically opened and closed her window. I dismounted from the bus in Zipolite into a blast of humidity and dust, prompting a resolution to never wear pants again, and headed to a cheap hotel in the Roca Blanca neighborhood at the western end of the beach. Perks of the room included a water pump under the floor that was not unlike a jackhammer in its effects on the immediate environment. I settled in to await Marwan's arrival.

On the surface, Zipolite—Mexico's only official clothing-optional beach—was not exactly my type of seaside, despite its aesthetic glory: a kilometer and a half of golden sand surrounded by hills that abruptly turn from brown to green with the (now erratic) arrival of the rainy season. But the fierce currents rendered swimming for sport or leisure essentially impossible, and even just wading in to pee often constituted a lengthy struggle. The iconic giant white rock off the coast—hence "Roca Blanca," rumored to be the result of accumulated bird shit—provided the backdrop for many a nude selfie, as well as many a photograph surreptitiously and not so surreptitiously captured by visitors from Mexico City on nudist safari. The panorama also played host to all manner of naked yoga, meditation, hula-hooping, acrobatics, jogging, and lounging. These activities posed a conundrum for me, because, try as I did to appreciate the participants' bucking of the silly convention of clothing, white people doing yoga naked was somehow even more irritating than white people doing yoga clothed, and I usually just ended up feeling like a reactionary asshole. Until, that is, the quarantine happened and there was no longer a surplus of people to throw me into ethical dilemmas.

A village of only a few thousand inhabitants, Zipolite's clientele ranged from the aforementioned demographics to gay vacationers to Mexican families from surrounding towns to surfers, drug enthusiasts, older European couples who conducted morning strolls on the beach in matching straw hats, and ever well-behaved compatriots of mine—like the woman whose life I ruined by taking too long to pay at the convenience store and who entered into an apoplectic fit in the way that only Americans know how. Canadians fleeing their dismal climate were also in abundance, and a Canadian-specific condominium complex called La Monarca—a yellow monstrosity responsible for the devastation of a coastal mangrove—was the predominant eyesore among the otherwise largely unobtrusive architecture (think non-yellow hotels, thatched roof huts, cabins, hammocks).

Marwan joined the water pump and me in Roca Blanca on March 15, the day the Associated Press issued the following report on the Mexican coronavirus front: "AMLO Shakes, Hugs, Cheek-kisses Despite Virus Advice." Three days later, the headline "AMLO Defies Virus Worry With Hugs and Kisses at Mexico Oil Bash" accompanied a *Bloomberg* write-up of the celebration at Pemex headquarters in Mexico City marking the anniversary of the 1938 nationalization of the Mexican oil industry. AMLO, of course, was leftist Mexican president Andrés Manuel López Obrador, who had assumed office in 2018 and was not racking up any points in terms of heeding current health precautions. (Nor was he racking up points in terms of his promise to refrain from performing the anti-migrant dirty work of the imperial ruler to the north, which naturally became even dirtier in the context of the pandemic. He would, however, stick it to the empire in other ways, as when Walmart de México was forced to pay some $359 million in back taxes for the 2014 sale of its Vips restaurant chain—one of a slew of in-your-face victories against corporate tax dodging that would hit Coca-Cola bottler Femsa, too. As part of his "post-neoliberal" program, AMLO had furthermore rescued Pemex from the unpopular privatization experiment conducted by his right-wing predecessor Enrique Peña Nieto, while also significantly slashing his own salary and flying economy class.) As media reports of his counter-social-distancing measures spiked, AMLO took the opportunity at a news conference to display the amulets he said were protecting him from the virus. A studious avoider of face masks, the Mexican leader would eventually commit in late July to donning a mask and ceasing to speak only when corruption had been eradicated in the country, i.e., presumably not prior to the self-destruction of the human race.

This pledge was made just as Mexico overtook the United Kingdom to account for the third-most COVID fatalities globally. To be sure, as with many a crisis on Mexican soil over the years, the U.S. bore no small part of the blame for the gravity of the coronavirus fallout. Consider, for example, the toxic effects of the 1994

North American Free Trade Agreement on the Mexican diet ("free trade" being the euphemism for the United States' freedom to wreak economic havoc as it pleases and everyone else's freedom to suck it up). Diabetes and obesity levels soared, ultimately putting Mexico and the U.S. neck-and-neck for the title of world's most obese population and, now, increasing the risk of COVID mortality. Mexicans consume more soda per capita than any other country on the planet; former Mexican president Vicente Fox was once the CEO of Coca-Cola Mexico. Indeed, Coca-Cola is so ubiquitously present—and effectively pushed down people's throats by relentless advertising campaigns—that one is liable to conclude it's the national beverage. In August 2020, the state of Oaxaca would be the first to ban the sale of junk food and sugary drinks to children under the age of eighteen, a law endorsed by Mexico's Assistant Health Secretary and coronavirus czar Hugo López-Gatell, who had incurred industrial wrath by denouncing soda as "bottled poison."

At the time of Marwan's arrival to Oaxaca on the ides of March, López-Gatell had just announced the impending *Jornada Nacional de la Sana Distancia*—"National Day of Social Distancing"—which ended up lasting from March 23 until May 30. A coronavirus cumbia that would quickly come to inundate radio waves similarly endowed the pandemic with a semi-festive air, with its upbeat reminders to frequently wash hands and use disinfectant because *"es muy efectivo."* Face masks were yet to be seen in Zipolite though, and as Marwan and I were under the impression that we would soon be traveling to Mexico City and then to landlocked Mérida on the Yucatán Peninsula, we took advantage of the time to park ourselves uselessly in the sand with an arsenal of wine. Sometimes, experiences came to us, as when a policeman arrived on an all-terrain vehicle to inquire if Marwan was the person who had just drowned. Given Marwan's lack of Spanish, I had replied, as one does: "But he's not even wet," and the policeman had moved on to interrogate the next person. Writing the encounter off as just your typical magical-realist moment rather than an indication of the perils of this particular stretch of sea, I would certainly recall it months later following my near-fatal collision with the wave and discovery re: *playa de la muerte*.

I had known Marwan since May 25, 2013, the date easily rememberable as it was the thirteenth anniversary of the Israeli withdrawal from south Lebanon after twenty-two years of military occupation. I was en route from Latin America to the hypercapitalist dystopia of the United Arab Emirates and had stopped over in Beirut, one of my regular destinations since 2006, when Amelia and I had spent a couple of months hitchhiking through the rubble of the aftermath of that summer's assault by Israel. Marwan's mother was from the Gaza Strip, where, thanks to Israeli policies of territorial control and ethnic cleansing, Marwan was barred from setting foot; his uncle, a top intelligence aide to Yasser Arafat, had been assassinated by the Mossad in Paris in 1992. Our 2020 reunion in Zipolite gave us the chance to reminisce about previous joint excursions—such as the time I dragged Marwan hitchhiking in south Lebanon near the Israeli border only to be deported from the area by a pair of men in a shiny car, who had with disproportionate enthusiasm introduced themselves as the Lebanese equivalent of the FBI. Our transgression, allegedly, was having sneaked through an (unmanned) army checkpoint that was in part designed to keep foreigners without the proper permission—i.e., me—out of the immediate border region. In reality, it seemed there were sectarian issues at play involving Marwan's unmistakably Sunni surname, since the FBI had simply glanced at my passport and then darted across the street with his identity card and their walkie-talkies. I returned to the border the next day without him.

Checkpoints, as it so happened, would rapidly come to define my existence in Zipolite. Long before that, though, they were a defining feature of the Lebanese landscape, and had notoriously facilitated ID card–based sectarian killings during the civil war of 1975–90. Nowadays in Lebanon, their function is more to provide an illusion of security and competence on the part of the state, which continues to be dominated by civil warlords with massive amounts of blood on their hands and little concern for anything aside from their own stranglehold on power (hence the August 2020 mega-explosion that destroyed much of Beirut for no other reason than gross political negligence). In a country of eighteen recognized religious sects, where power is allocated according to the ostensible size of each group, the divide-and-conquer system helps perpetuate the stranglehold by ensuring the dependence of the masses on their respective confessional elite. Checkpoints can also, then, be instrumental in maintaining sectarian geographies—and the confessionalization of space—by reminding the Other of his or her outsider-ness. Socioeconomic boundaries, too, are enforced by checkpoints, as in the case of Beirut's postwar downtown. The space is an ode to nauseating wealth, where, if the average poor inhabitant of Lebanon is not already sufficiently repelled by the multimillion-dollar apartments and criminally expensive dining and shopping options, there's also a fluctuating arrangement of police, soldiers, cement barricades, barbed wire, and other obstacles to drive home the point that this is a militarized border between haves and have-nots.

Just across Lebanon's southern border, meanwhile, the Israelis take the cake for checkpoint-based criminalization. The military checkpoint is a pillar of Israel's repertoire of techniques for Making Life Hell for Palestinians, and, as Elia Zureik notes in an essay for the *Jerusalem Quarterly*,

> Body searches, identity documentation, standing in line for hours awaiting a signal from Israeli soldiers to either proceed or be turned away are emblematic of the checkpoint experience, which is characterized by dehumanization, lack of sovereignty, and overall limitation on free movement.

Over the years, Israel has strived to perfect its repressive technologies and conquer global security industry and surveillance markets accordingly, and checkpoints have proven handy testing grounds (as has Gaza, where the ability to periodically slaughter thousands of Palestinians while suffering negligible casualties in return surely speaks to the efficacy of one's armaments). But low-tech brutality is plentiful as well. In *Palestine Inside Out: An Everyday Occupation*, Saree Makdisi quotes thirty-one-year-old Abdallah Khamis on an attempt to return home via the Huwwara checkpoint near the West Bank city of Nablus, where he and his family had waited in line for three hours:

> The soldier pushed my wife with his hand, and I grabbed his hand. He tried to push her again. He and another soldier who was standing there grabbed me. One child was in my arms. The soldier took him from me and put him on the ground. One of them told me, in Arabic, "Go to the pen for those who are detained." I told

him, "I am not going anywhere. I am going to my house." They tried to bind my hands with plastic cuffs, and I resisted. Suddenly, one of the soldiers grabbed me by the ears while another soldier smashed my head on a concrete partition-wall. Another soldier hit me on the back of my head with his rifle butt.

Of course, it was nothing so dramatic when, in late March of 2020, coronavirus checkpoints were spontaneously erected on either side of Zipolite. The local assembly had voted to restrict entry to residents of the immediate vicinity and visitors who had been there for two weeks or more. Similar measures were taken throughout the region, and checkpoints began popping up everywhere. Marwan and I had just made the two-week cut, having skipped our flight to Mexico City on account of uncertainty as to the future of the world and general laziness. We were issued paper "Control COVID-19 Zipolite" IDs—I was number 236—a process that required excessive standing in a non-socially distanced line in the sun sans face masks, supervised by a policeman with hand sanitizer in his holster. With these IDs, we were permitted to travel once a week as far as the city of Pochutla, half an hour to the north, for groceries and banking. We were not permitted to travel to the beach town of Mazunte, fifteen minutes to the west, although intriguing loopholes would subsequently be reported. Some folks, for example, were allowed to leave their motorbikes at the checkpoint and cross on foot, inanimate objects being the obvious transmitters of coronavirus.

The Zipolite checkpoints were manned by a fluctuating array of civilian volunteers, policemen, and, finally, heavily armed Marines, when it was determined that the first two groups were inordinately focused on eating and not adequately intimidating to aspiring violators of the quarantine. "*Quédate en casa*" took off as the coronavirus rallying cry, and I was faced with the distinctly terrifying prospect of having to "stay at home" after nearly two decades without a fixed address or even country of residence. A mandatory curfew was not imposed, but the crowd in Zipolite began to disappear, hotels and restaurants closed, and I was overcome with a clichéd physical urge to run (which, mercifully, was now at least within the realm of possibility as I was no longer reduced to hopping). I was also well aware that having a nervous breakdown over being stuck on a pristine Pacific beach was rather less than charming in a world of actual problems.

For a couple of days I pursued my own version of *Quédate en casa*, which consisted of dispatching Marwan to the main cobblestone street in the center of Zipolite—one block back from the beach—to assess just how apocalyptically empty the scene was and whether I would be able to handle it. I took back my disparaging thoughts about naked yoga and naked hula-hooping. With each email update from my parents concerning their own genuine lockdown in Barcelona—and the number of times my dad had vacuumed the apartment that day—I accumulated vicarious feelings of incarceration and supplementary clichéd urges. Even the beach itself was transformed from a venue of psychological escape into a reminder of captivity when it was temporarily decided that sand and sea were closed for coronavirus and that soldiers and police would be tasked with chasing everyone off, while simultaneously photographing their chasing-off efforts for publicity purposes.

Inept at dealing with authority figures, I endeavored to conceal my terror—and neurotic visions of being banned from the ocean forevermore—by responding to evacuation orders with "*ahorita*," which, while technically meaning "right away" or "in a minute," can also be construed as a commitment to carrying out an act at some point in the future or maybe never. Marwan, having had his fair share of unpleasant run-ins with Lebanese law enforcement, was not a fan of this approach, and preferred to retreat from the beach as instructed; I inevitably followed, but not without plans to return. I was also developing a contingency plan, in the event that shit really hit the fan, which involved hiding in the woods by day and sneaking to the sea at night, where I would conceal myself under a mound of sand, undetectable by the flashing lights of the police patrols. (Fortunately, this strategy would not have to be carried out, as it was soon decided that the beach was not closed after all.)

As pleasant company as I undoubtedly was, Marwan's first order of quarantine business was to figure out how to get himself back to Lebanon, his job, his PhD program, and his ailing father. This was accomplished the second week of April, after the Lebanese embassy in Mexico City had informed him via WhatsApp that—while they were very sorry not to be able to invite him for a Lebanese feast during his stay in the country—it was now or maybe not until September if he wanted to get home. Although the taxi drivers of Zipolite were unsure as to whether it was even possible to get through the checkpoints to the airport in nearby Huatulco, the journey was a success, and Marwan embarked on a series of flights broken up by a multiday campout at Charles de Gaulle Airport in Paris. Appallingly, no wine whatsoever was available in said airport, which was most troubling to a Japanese traveler who had spent ten days making his way from Angola to France via Algeria and was now scheduled for a weeklong wait in the terminal before his coronavirus repatriation flight. In the end, Marwan reported, appeals to airport staff and security officials were fruitless, and the Japanese made do with meditation.

I, on the other hand, had access to far too much wine for my own good, not to mention beer and mezcal, despite the COVID-19 alcohol ban that had officially been implemented by the municipality of Pochutla. In Zipolite, the ban was half-assed. For instance, at the corner convenience store that, depending on which side of the building you consulted, was called either Abarrotes Vicky or Abarrotes Bety, the ban initially meant that beer was openly available only until 6 p.m.—and after that only if you had a bag to hide it in. As the quarantine dragged on, the store began selling solely on the sly, and then not at all. At several other shops in town, however, it was business entirely as usual—which enabled me to continue to rely on alcohol consumption as a pseudo-solution for how to keep running away from myself while stuck in one place.

I rented an apartment for an unspecified period on the eastern edge of town, the opposite end from Roca Blanca, in the Playa del Amor neighborhood, named for a small but magnificent beach just over the hill that was reachable by staircase. At this beach—one of the advantages of which was that the police couldn't be bothered to climb the stairs—I spent many mornings lying on a rock atop a blanket I had pilfered from Turkish Airlines and trying not to feel body-shamed by Claudio, the older, overly fit Italian who utilized the area to perfect his collection of abdominal muscles. My apartment was approximately three minutes walking from the Playa del Amor staircase, and a shorter distance from Abarrotes Vicky and/or Bety. It was an even shorter distance than that from the newly installed checkpoint on the road to the fishing village of Puerto Ángel, four kilometers away, beyond which lay Pochutla and more checkpoints. Hovering over my apartment was an advertisement for Corona beer, lest anyone try to forget for a moment the current theme of the world.

My new home, which doubled as a furnace even with all windows left perpetually open, was painted yellow and white on the inside and came equipped with the basic necessities: bed, table, fridge, portable gas stove, oscillating fan (otherwise known as salvation), and a July 2005 magazine courtesy of the now-defunct Mexicana Airlines spotlighting an Orthodox wedding in Israel. Domestic wildlife included lizards, spiders, mosquitoes, cockroaches, the occasional scorpion, and the iguana I found peering down at me from a hole in the ceiling as I arose from a nap and who nearly cost me my coronary functions. I quickly adopted a policy of coexistence with ants—complete with right to freedom of assembly and food sharing—which applied insofar as they stayed out of bodily orifices. Outside the apartment, there was a fairly continuous crowing of roosters day and night, mixed with sounds of reggaetón, ranchera music, the coronavirus cumbia, and whatever else was on the neighbors' radios, plus the ever-present crash of waves. In the mornings, there was also the sound of sweeping, a primary matutinal ritual in Zipolite, where pretty much everything was eligible to be swept: home, sidewalk, street, beach, dirt. (As much as I dreamed of becoming one of these morning sweepers, it remained an unfulfilled fantasy.) When in early May the Puerto Ángel checkpoint relocated from down the road to directly in front of my house, the soundscape became more variegated.

There was no water in the shower, so bathing required filling buckets from the trickle that emerged from the kitchen sink. For this purpose I purchased two plastic buckets, one green and one pink, for a total of three dollars, an act that unforeseeably unleashed an obsessive-compulsive bucket-buying habit. I bought a bucket to wash clothes; I bought another to wash the Turkish Airlines blanket. I bought yet another to wash cleaning rags. I bought a blue bucket and a purple bucket to give to a neighbor, but then kept them because they were pretty. I bought buckets to carry fruit and vegetables, and buckets to store water for whenever there was none or I didn't feel like spending half my life washing a fork under the tap. The buckets were acquired at the same shop in Zipolite where I had attempted to buy chicken feed, mistaking it for some exotic indigenous grain and occasioning an intervention by the shop proprietor, who had charitably put an end to my White Person Spectacle.

The buckets were covered in dirt and unidentifiable filth when I acquired them, and themselves had to be scrubbed prior to use. Their handles were rusted, the standard fate of metal objects in the salty air of Zipolite. Part of the buckets' appeal was that they transported me back to a scene in a remote hamlet in Morocco in 2005, where Amelia and I had hitchhiked to visit the family of our friend Abdul. I had met Amelia upon abandoning the U.S. in 2003, when we were both enrolled in a certification course in Crete to teach English as a foreign language. Teaching aspirations had been swiftly discarded in favor of cross-continental hitchhiking expeditions interspersed with for-profit activity, such as stints at an avocado-packing facility in an Andalusian village in southern Spain, where Abdul worked in construction and inexplicably invited us to reside rent-free in his house.

In retrospect, it seems remarkable that Amelia and I made it to Abdul's family's home—located somewhere in the central Béni Mellal-Khénifra region—with nothing more than an extremely vague concept of Moroccan geography, some handwritten notes by Abdul, and the immeasurable benevolence of motorists, who were never quite sure why it was that we needed to reach this remote hamlet but went at times hours out of their way to get us there, inevitably plying us along the way with euphoria-inducing tea, bread, olive oil, and other reasons to despair over industrial food production. More euphoria was on hand courtesy of Abdul's extended family, although the limits were tested by five consecutive days of nonstop ingestion. Abdul's numerous sisters—when not arranging the latest tray of comestibles, participating in impromptu dance parties as we made the rounds of relatives' houses, or dressing Amelia and me up in their nightgowns—were forever occupied with buckets, in which water from the well was alternately carried to the bathroom, kitchen, sheep pen, or whatever surface was in need of cleaning. Hence the Orientalist bucket nostalgia nearly fifteen years later, as I swung my pink bucket romantically around my Zipolite apartment and imagined myself a Moroccan peasant.

At the outset of his travelogue *A Stranger's Pose*, Nigerian writer Emmanuel Iduma describes driving into Mauritania at sunset during the Eid al-Fitr holiday as men are strolling home from the mosque: "I am moved by these swaggering bodies, dressed in their finest, walking to houses that look only seven feet high. I envy the ardor in their gait, a lack of hurry, as if by walking they possess a piece of the earth . . . I want to be these men." This is pretty much the story of my life—except that, not only do I want to be the Mauritanian mosque men, I want to be everyone everywhere at all times. For me, Abdul's sisters with their buckets possessed a piece of the earth: a solidity and assuredness of existence—in spite of economic precariousness—that was unavailable to me as I darted about the globe in privileged incoherence, endeavoring to conduct myriad parallel lives against different backdrops but possessing no piece of earth or coherent identity in the process. There was a simple grace in this solidity that I could not aspire to, although the Zipolite bucket fixation did permit me to briefly pretend I was the most domesticated, settled person ever, while also providing a welcome distraction from planetary calamity. Domestication reached new heights with the acquisition of a mop, a hammock, a glittery hand-painted mug, and not one but two candles decorated with Day of the Dead skulls.

Of course, the novelty of a sedentary lifestyle would quickly wear off, and I'd find myself racing in circles around the Zipolite soccer field in a bid to placate the jinn that had detected optimal prey in my idle self. To sustain the illusion of movement, I would traipse up and down the beach, intermittently thwarted by the police, who had undergone a wardrobe change in honor of coronavirus and were now rocking fancy blue outfits instead of white shirts and shorts. They had also gotten their hands on a siren, which was fitted onto one of the all-terrain vehicles before a stroke of great fortune caused the siren to disappear. When I had to run errands in Roca Blanca at the other end of the beach, like stock up on vegetables and gratuitous quantities of Oaxaca cheese, I'd sometimes pretend I was voyaging to another country—a vain effort to stretch as far as possible the smattering of kilometers to which my world had shrunk. I tried to ground my thoughts, and to accept that it was, like, okay to be still for a bit in a place where footwear was not needed under any circumstances and that was, objectively speaking, ludicrously beautiful. (And where else would running errands involve stumbling upon nude solo boxing performances and nude lunging?) But wandering barefoot in paradise was somehow not sufficient to keep my mind in place rather than ricocheting between Tajikistan, Paraguay, Cambodia, and all of the other lands I had been once upon a time and could now not go.

Nor was it just a manic carousel of countries, cities, people, and slabs of Georgian khachapuri flashing through my head. There was also an element of corporeal agony attending the schizophrenic trip down memory lane. As in, I felt an actual surge of physical anguish with each recollection—and the more trivial the recollection, evidently, the greater the suffering. On one occasion, for instance, I woke up in the middle of the night weeping about the escalator (yes, escalator) that transports the Sarajevo grocery shopper from road level to the Konzum supermarket below ground. (This just across Marshal Tito Street from a monument to children killed during the siege of the city in the early nineties.) On another, sobbing convulsions were triggered by the memory of a certain kitchen knife at my friend's apartment in Fethiye, Turkey, where I had been a constant guest since 2004 and where a good portion of my worldly possessions continued to reside. There were tears for my clunky room key in Isfahan and the frigid stairwell in Bishkek, for exhaust fumes at the bus terminal in the northern Ethiopian city of Shire and for the Istanbul airport bathroom where I regularly opened duty-free wine with a plastic corkscrew I had obtained in Uzbekistan.

Tears were also elicited by my international collection of plastic bags—another of my weaknesses, the ecological recklessness of which I semi-atoned for by never throwing them away. Konzum had a nice green-and-red one, albeit less nice when the dye began to run and destroy other items in my suitcase. My Armenian, Lebanese, and Spanish plastic bags were utilized for carrying my packages of yerba mate, yerba mate gourds, and other yerba mate equipment, while the Italian plastic bag was for flip-flops, the Iranian plastic bag functioned as a purse, and the EgyptAir plastic bag was for a dress I never wore but carted around everywhere nonetheless. (There were also endless plastic bags of lesser sentimental value, used for preventing damage from olive oil spills and other potential havoc wreaked by materials incompatible with peregrination.) The ongoing emotional tragedy occasioned by being physically stuck was, however, somewhat assuaged by a recurring nightmare in which the Mexicans deported me to the U.S.—in light of which all other earthly eventualities became relatively benign in nature and *Quédate en casa* began to sound like an almost marvelous idea.

I say relatively benign because, on the yerba mate front, the quarantine produced quite the quagmire. I was still surviving off of the stash I had brought with me from Barcelona to San Salvador and had been planning to restock in Mérida, where Marwan and I were meant to be headed after Zipolite and where I knew from experience that it was easily accessible. Amelia and I had gotten hooked on mate while hitchhiking in 2006 in Syria and Lebanon, where Arab migration to and from South America had been responsible for the arrival of the beverage; when my parents then moved from the U.S. to Buenos Aires for some years, my addiction was cemented. Amelia had since married a Mexican man from the state of Puebla and moved to Mérida, hence its inclusion on the 2020 itinerary-that-wasn't.

I initially assumed I could resolve the yerba mate supply problem by simply ordering it on the internet for delivery like a normal person. This was before I learned that the mindfuck of having a fixed address after being on the move for almost two decades was even more of a mindfuck, because I didn't actually have an address at all. When informed of this by the landlady—whose texted response to my request for the apartment's *dirección* was *"Hola Belén, híjole! No hay direcciones"*—I set about gathering what I considered to be more-than-sufficient indications to guide any delivery van: GPS coordinates, Google map codes, relevant landmarks, house and foliage descriptions, and even a promise of ice-cold refreshment upon delivery for good measure.

At the end of April, I conceded defeat. By this point, I was on crying emoji terms with the girl at the miniscule DHL office in Pochutla, who, while sympathetic to my plight, could do nothing to align the universe to allow yerba mate-laden vehicles coming from Oaxaca City or Huatulco to cross the requisite checkpoints to get to me. I spent hours in online negotiations with customer service representatives of Amazon México, who were similarly amicably impotent. A Canadian friend attempted to DHL a package of mate from Ontario to Pochutla, only to have it detained forevermore at customs in Mexico City. Meanwhile, I engaged in racial profiling and accosted some people advertising Argentine empanadas on the beach, who agreed to part with half a kilo of Rosamonte-brand yerba mate for five dollars, which bought me an extra week.

In the end, the only sustainable solution was to somehow make it to the Super Chedraui of Huatulco, an hour and a half from Zipolite, where unlike at the Super Chedraui of Pochutla it was possible to place an order for yerba mate pickup. It was not possible to know if I'd be let through all the checkpoints on the way there, or, if let through, if I'd then be let back. I set out one morning with a young taxi driver friend named Miguel, who was also studying to be a teacher—whenever, that is, the Zipolite internet connection did not prove an insurmountable obstacle to remote pandemic learning—and who filled me in on the latest coronavirus gossip during our ride. Thus far, there were no reported cases of the virus in the village, but Pochutla was said to have between zero and three, while the number of conspiracy theories was infinite. One theory, according to Miguel, involved the chupacabras, although my mind was not advanced enough to grasp the specifics. Another rumor, he reported, was that the government had paid off the doctor of a young girl who had died of cancer to write up the death as a COVID fatality and disappear the body—for what reason no one was really sure, beyond the assumption that, since the government had always lied about everything else, coronavirus must be a lie, too.

And so it was that—eight coronavirus checkpoints, one coronavirus car fumigation, one police interrogation of Miguel, and two near-martyrdoms of iguanas on the highway later—I was standing conquistador-style over a mound of yerba mate packages on my kitchen table. The interrogating officer had kept my Zipolite coronavirus ID at the Huatulco checkpoint while Miguel and I made the run to Super Chedraui, where the staff had politely looked on as I embraced the mound and loaded it into my assorted Armenian plastic bags.

At home with my treasure, I felt that life could, at least for the moment, go on. This was a far more optimistic outlook than would be espoused exactly two weeks later, when the decision was made to relocate the Zipolite–Puerto Ángel checkpoint to my front yard—where the first order of business was to prevent me from *entering* my house without a face mask, impassioned appeals to logic notwithstanding.

Halfway through *Zorba the Greek*, Nikos Kazantzakis's narrator receives a letter from "a mountain somewhere in Tanganyika," sent by an old schoolmate called Karayannis. Formerly a professor of theology, Karayannis had absconded to Africa after hooking up with a female student. Sitting alone on a stone in Crete, the narrator reads the letter and reflects: "Once again I felt flashing inside me the urge to leave, not owing to any need—since I am fine on this seashore where I comfortably fit in and lack nothing—but owing to my compelling desire to see and touch as much sea and land as possible before I die."

At the start of the quarantine, I had decided to reread *Zorba* in an unimaginative tribute to the fact that I was supposed to have traveled to Greece in

May. The golden sand and crashing waves of Zipolite served as the backdrop for my reading-slash-mental-boomeranging between other lands and seas, even as I lacked nothing on this seashore aside from immunity to periodic eviction by Mexican soldiers and police. In my case, the seeing and touching of everything was also a convenient way to postpone sorting my shit out or committing to a single identity, as the constant motion enabled a suspension of conventional reality and the illusion, at least, of an elongation of time, into which I endeavored to cram as much land and sea as possible between myself and mortality. Since the onset of my travels in 2003, I had become more comfortable with the idea of one day ceasing to exist, a prospect that had disproportionately preoccupied my childhood in Washington, DC, and Austin, Texas—to the extent that I would remain awake at night calculating the number of years/hours/minutes I might reasonably have left based on current American life expectancy. In the evenings, I could be found lying in rigid petrification on the living room rug, imagining myself inside a coffin while my parents watched the newscast. It's possible that I simply associated death with failure in the prevailing context of cutthroat capitalism; after all, I could not be the best, most successful student and person ever if I was dead. At any rate, the peripatetic urges that were to consume me later in life would provide a welcome distraction from morbid fixation.

It was during the period of *Zorba* and beach confrontations with police that I met Javier, a diminutive near-septuagenarian sporting a modified mullet and old red undershirt, who, installed in a plastic chair by the water, remained unmoved by the exhortations of the forces of law and order. Firm in his spot, he sipped mezcal from a plastic bottle, chain-smoked, and wrote meticulously in a notebook he kept in a large Ziploc bag, itself kept inside a blue-and-gray handwoven bag. Desperate for some of the permanence and security exuded by this man, I crept over to him one evening after the police had once again chased me off. Javier explained good-naturedly that, while he understood that the cops were simply doing their job, both they and the coronavirus could *chingar a su madre*. From then on, I pitched my Turkish Airlines blanket next to his chair in the evenings.

Hailing from Cuernavaca in the central Mexican state of Morelos, Javier had been a regular in Zipolite since the famed solar eclipse of 1970, which had coincidentally taken place on my birthday, March 7. Since 1982, coincidentally my birth year, he had owned a small plot of land on a hill, where we would subsequently plant corn, beans, and squash (or rather, where I would get my rustic farming fix by following Javier's instructions for a few minutes on which seeds to drop in which holes). He also ran a small auto parts shop, called El Sol, which was located across from the soccer field where I conducted morning jinn expulsions and whose most official address was "Autopartes El Sol, across from the soccer field," as I confirmed during my frantic survey of yerba mate delivery options. Javier divided his time between Zipolite and Morelos, where his wife, a sociologist, held down the fort, but his scheduled return home in early April had been thwarted on account of the pandemic and the cancellation of his flight. His idea to ride his motorbike instead for more than seven hundred kilometers had been shot down by his sons, both academics in Mexico City, who reminded him of the arbitrary nature of the checkpoint regime and the likelihood of ending up trapped in the middle of nowhere. His wife, for her part, would over the ensuing months grow increasingly unimpressed with his poetic text messages of *inmensa gratitud*—usually accompanied by his preferred seedling emoji—and narrated cell phone videos of surf and sky.

Javier's gratitude became ever more immense in accordance with mezcal and marijuana consumption, and he would spend much of the night saluting the stars, moon, and sea—to which he committedly referred in its feminine form, *la mar.* There was gratitude for all the people who had smiled at him that day, from the young girl on the street to the older woman on the beach with whom he had shared a brief exchange of meteorological predictions to the motorcycle repairman, who had been one of many recipients of unsolicited mango delivery. (As he had recently discovered, randomly gifting people mangoes was an easy way to earn smiles.) There was gratitude for the hummingbird that had visited him as he was watering his bougainvillea, and for AMLO, who was nobly wresting Mexico from the grip of the *hijos de la chingada*—an undertaking Javier reckoned was even more difficult with one's mouth covered, leading him to wholeheartedly endorse the presidential aversion to face masks. Javier was additionally grateful to AMLO for expediting pension payments during the coronavirus crisis—although there were plenty of critics who said the government wasn't doing nearly enough to facilitate the survival of the most vulnerable Mexicans—and defended the president's attendance at a mid-pandemic meeting in Washington with Donald Trump to celebrate NAFTA's new and improved iteration.

(At the bilateral July encounter, Trump was commended for uncharacteristically good behavior.) AMLO's participation, Javier insisted, was not a bout of neoliberal ass-kissing; rather, it was a calculated move to keep the gringos happily distracted and not *chingando* while he went about reinventing Mexico behind their back.

I myself was also repeatedly on the receiving end of Javier's thanks—and not only for introducing red wine into the mix of mind-altering substances, which had earned me some lines in the Ziplocked notebook, e.g., "*Belén vino, con su vino*" ("Belén came, with her wine"). Turning to me with an expression of wonder that the life he had lived had really been his, and as though watching a rerun of it play out in the space between us, Javier would dispense *gracias* upon *gracias* for bringing to mind memories he hadn't thought of in decades— like the time in the 1970s his *abuela* in Cuernavaca, who had taken in stride his decision to abandon an impending professional soccer career in favor of mushrooms and other activities, had given him a Volkswagen and a blender to go make smoothies in Zipolite. On the drive south from Oaxaca City, the car had flipped and Javier had ended up in a ditch, from which he was extricated by a woman waiting at a bus stop. The moral of the story, according to Javier's *abuela*: the woman had been an angel.

The same buoyant optimism applied to his recounting of other episodes, such as the one in which he had sustained a severe head injury falling off a Zipolite rooftop while urinating in the middle of the night. Even the devastating Mexico City earthquake of 1985, for which casualty estimates ranged from horrific to even more horrific, had a bright side, and Javier recalled the human solidarity that had been on display—primarily, he said, among rescue volunteers of the fifteen to twenty-five age range, and excluding the people in the government. Now, the coronavirus constituted another opportunity for human improvement, and Javier foresaw the cultivation of a better, more just and equitable post-pandemic world that was not managed by *hijos de la chingada*, although it annoyed him when I asked for the details of how maladies like capitalism and climate change were to be suddenly rectified when capitalism thrived on mass suffering in the first place. Sometimes, his annoyance would abate, and he would admit that our sitting and staring at the sea was perhaps not the most hands-on approach to revolution.

As Javier liked to repeat, he was a great fan of Octavio Paz's musings on the immeasurable uses of *chingar*—a "magical word," Paz writes in *The Labyrinth of Solitude*. This did not mean that Javier discriminated against other popular Mexican vulgarities. "*No mames*" was a frequent rebuttal when he'd had enough of my insistence that the world was irreparably shitty; it was also the response to another white chick who approached Javier in my absence and inquired if he was a shaman. "*Pinche Javier, estás loco, cabrón*" was meanwhile reportedly his response to himself when he awoke at sunrise to find himself curled up next to the remains of a fire he made on the beach the night before. Although Javier was generally mild-mannered even in his effusiveness, my choice of reading materials conditioned me to detect Zorba-esque moments, as when he would break into song or spontaneously perform a headstand.

The arrival of the checkpoint to my front yard was a new occasion for the deployment of Octavio Paz's magical word and many others. I also managed a *Zorba the Greek* parallel when, barred from entering my apartment without a mask and shouted at by Toño—the stocky *agente municipal* carrying out his two-year term as overlord of the village assembly, where the decision had been taken in March to institute the checkpoint regime—I imagined myself the Cretan widow being pursued by the bloodthirsty mob of villagers. The day was May 11. Sometime around midmorning, I'd heard a ruckus and looked out my window to discover a crowd of civilians and police erecting an encampment of tarps, plastic chairs, water barrels, and coronavirus signage. Still not putting two and two together, I opened the front door to find a thick rope stretched across the road, one end of which was held by a volunteer who cheerfully communicated to me that, following complaints from neighbors down the road, the checkpoint had officially been moved here. My first thought was how, given my lack of curtains, I would now have to wear clothes inside—certainly high up there on the list of global coronavirus tragedies. My second, related, thought was that my life was over.

I ran, disheveled, to the beach, where, sure enough, Javier was ensconced in his plastic chair and had gotten into the mezcal earlier than usual. I dropped my Turkish Airlines blanket next to him, bleating unintelligibly about tarps and ropes and surveillance and captivity. He attempted to execute one of his signature longwinded hugs—complete with sniffing of my neck—before being reminded about social distancing, and I dashed to the water's edge to stare into oblivion. Once a sufficiently dramatic period of time had elapsed,

I returned to Javier, who had resolved to accompany me back to my apartment in order to convey a message to the checkpoint folk: "*No chinguen.*"

By now the checkpoint was in full swing, and had amassed an even larger crowd on account of it being mealtime (indeed, there was some speculation that free food was the raison d'être of the whole shebang). And it was now that the face mask–front door scene went down. From behind a mound of rice and beans, his own mask resting on his chin, Toño barked orders for Javier and me to halt. It mattered not that I was approximately four meters from my doorstep; I was not going another step without a face mask. As Javier sputtered through his lexicon of curses, I endeavored to stave off an aneurysm while making the following points:

1. If by some crazy coincidence I was the only person in Zipolite to have coronavirus, I would be doing much more harm to the *pueblo* outside my house than in it.

2. No one in Zipolite wore a face mask except at the checkpoint, including Toño and all of the others manning it. For pedestrians and motorists alike, checkpoint-crossing etiquette consisted of pausing during approach to don the face mask and then removing it once the obstacle had been cleared.

A policeman eventually took me aside, gave me a disposable mask, and told me to wear it within ten meters of the rope, after which the need expired. This was the same policeman who would, on the second night of the checkpoint's presence, spearhead the operation to move the giant grill positioned beneath my window to a location less conducive to flooding my apartment with smoke, seconding my argument that it was wrong to protect me from coronavirus only to kill me by asphyxiation. Toño, for his part, managed to un-bunch his panties slightly and inaugurate an inexplicable tradition of soliciting swimming lessons whenever he saw me, and I gradually grew accustomed to having to step over a rope every time I went outside and being interrogated about my alleged *novio* and reproduction plans. The cops, who were being made to work twenty-four-plus-hour shifts, were bored out of their minds and took every opportunity to intercept me, whether to threaten to come drink beer at my house or to conduct impromptu Spanish vocabulary quizzes ("What is the name of that?" "Palm tree." "And that?" "Squirrel." "And that?" "Coronavirus megaphone with built-in foghorn"). Every sound I made—from washing dishes to flushing the toilet to crying over Turkish telenovelas to bellowing standard obscenities at my computer— was made with the awareness of having a permanent audience. Granted, there were various perks to the checkpoint arrangement, like the time I needed a jar of hot sauce opened, or a wasp slain—a feat requiring two policemen, one civilian, and a frisbee—or a coconut whacked with a machete. The latter weapon served other purposes, as well, and I once glanced out the window to see a checkpoint volunteer getting down to the coronavirus cumbia with machete as dance partner.

One evening shortly after the near-asphyxiation, I emerged from my apartment to find a man of about sixty passed out drunk in the yard, where he had ostensibly been assisting in guarding the village frontier against penetration by lethal microbes. In the interest of not being super gringa, I said nothing and proceeded to the beach, where Javier was waiting with some garlic chicken he had prepared and more memories he had unearthed. Among them was a hitchhiking trip in the 1970s with a friend, when they had been imprisoned for a few days in Puebla for drug possession—a demonstrably false charge, Javier maintained, because all drugs had been disposed of prior to the arrival of the police, who had carried out the arrest purely to *chingar*. As it turned out, though, even being jailed had its splendid side, and Javier recalled with *inmensa gratitud* the courtesy with which the other inmates had treated him and his friend. It was so enjoyable, in fact, that he hadn't wanted to leave, and upon being forcibly discharged had returned to Cuernavaca with an implacable nostalgia for life behind bars.

During our own hitchhiking days, the closest Amelia and I had come to imprisonment was in 2009 on the Colombian-Ecuadorian border, where we were accused of overstaying our permitted time in Colombia as we attempted to leave to Ecuador. We actually hadn't overstayed at all, having gone from Colombia to Venezuela for a month and then returned. However, we had no way of proving this, as we hadn't been able to locate anyone with passport-stamping capabilities on the Colombian-Venezuelan frontier and had thus flowed freely into the Bolivarian Republic and back—just like narcotics, terrorists, and other preferred existential menaces of imperial U.S. fantasy. The Colombians gave us the choice of detention or a bribe, which we negotiated down to what we would easily have spent in a day were we not hitchhiking and staying with benevolent strangers or in two-dollar-per-night truck-driver motels. As for Javier's attachment to his carceral experience, I had heard a similar sentiment years before—albeit from a friend who had spent more than a few days locked up. Having a Palestinian father and Lebanese mother, Hassan was, like many Palestinians in Lebanon, denied basic rights and barred from a multitude of jobs. After participating as a militant in the struggle against the Israeli occupation of south Lebanon, which ended in 2000, and undergoing several near-death incidents while trying to reach Europe, he had been interned for two years in Lebanon's notorious Roumieh prison for, inter alia, a scheme involving fake cement and a fake Somali ambassador. Though the conditions were unspeakable, he told me later, there was nonetheless something reassuring about being trapped and exempt from making decisions about life.

After listening to Javier's ode to incarceration and other tales, I returned to my own situation of confinement behind the checkpoint to learn that the previously passed-out man was now conscious and had opted to defecate on my doorstep. Two policemen tore themselves away from their cell phones to impose law and order, which they did first and foremost by decreeing that the man wipe up the mess with his shirt. This only caused the circumference of the pile to expand, sending the police back to the drawing board. A replacement solution was devised, which entailed dispatching the man to fetch a family member to come perform cleaning duties. Predictably, this resulted in him stumbling off down the road and never returning. The final solution of the night was to shovel dirt onto the excreta and wait until *mañana*.

The arrival of *mañana* brought no new ideas. Then, as I stood in the yard despairing over the circumstances, who should stroll by but the culprit himself. Now sober, he had no recollection of the episode, but took the collective word for it and agreeably got to work with the Clorox. Once he had finished and gone on his way, Toño presented me with a cookie and a reminder about swimming lessons, and we all lived happily ever after—until, that is, I almost ceased to live on account of a wave. This grand mishap transpired one fine afternoon in May, during an excursion to the beach that was preceded by a warning from four different people in the span of three minutes re: the sea's particular savagery that day.

I had the beach largely to myself, since Javier was putting in some hours at his auto parts shop and since it was hot as fuck in the middle of a quarantine. The police had given up on chasing people away, but there weren't many left to be chased in the first place. I was thus mercifully without spectators as I marched into the ocean and looked up to find what was not so much a wave as a supernatural wall of water bearing down on me. In the manner of a cartoon character that remains suspended in midair before realizing they've run off a cliff and plunging accordingly, I felt time stop just long enough for me to contemplate the magnitude of my imbecility before being hurtled backward with a force heretofore never imagined. In the midst of my high-speed tumble

I had many important thoughts, such as that my parents had spent a lot of money on me for nothing and that I would never again have sex because I'd be either paralyzed or dead. I slammed into the shore.

By some miracle, my neck didn't snap, and damage appeared to consist mainly of scrapes, raw skin, and the accumulation in every orifice of preposterous quantities of sand. After darting in and out of the sea once more just to show nature that it would not have the last word against the American, I slunk home, donning my face mask en route, and, stepping over the rope, navigated the gaggle of humans and stray dogs separating me from my front door and the vat of wine I had auto-prescribed. Of course, there's no point in almost dying if you can't whine to someone about it, so I emailed a friend in the States, who immediately referred me to the book *Say Her Name* by Francisco Goldman, whose young wife Aura Estrada was killed in 2007 by a wave in nearby Mazunte. Perusing the snippets of the book that I was allowed to view on the Amazon website, I arrived at the following line: "Zipolite is called la Playa de la Muerte because every year there are so many fatalities there." I downed the rest of my vat and wondered if I was really still alive.

When I later told Javier about the *playa de la muerte* designation, he was borderline offended by the idea that his beloved beach might be associated with mortality—although he did admit to having once been sitting by the water at night and seeing a crowd of shapes go by that were definitely not from among the living. In addition to the line from the Goldman book, I presented Javier with various tidbits found via a cursory search on the internet, such as the claim that "Zipolite" literally meant *playa de la muerte* in some indigenous language (there being disagreement as to whether this language was Zapotec, Mixtec, or Nahuatl). Eventually, he came around to the possibility that the designation was legit, but only after reasoning that, in the end, death was a celebration in Mexico: "We even have mariachis, *cabrón*."

Granted, the pandemic had made dying considerably less fun, as discussed in an *El País* article of May 31 headlined "*La muerte ya no es una fiesta*"—or "death isn't a party anymore." One of the article's protagonists, sixty-three-year-old Guillermo Patiño, alias El Frijol (The Bean), had worked half a century as a mariachi and had rarely seen Plaza Garibaldi—Mexico City's mariachi hub—so empty. Due to coronavirus measures, El Frijol and his band were barred from entering cemeteries, and they had played only one wake all month—in the poor barrio of Iztapalapa, with face masks, and in abridged form: *guitarrón*, *vihuela*, trumpet, and two violins, because "now with *sana distancia* they won't let ten mariachis in the funeral parlor."

In July, my friend Amelia's grandmother-in-law died of coronavirus in a town in Puebla, not far from Mexico City. Amelia wrote me that the family "couldn't help themselves" and summoned mariachis to the house, where the cousins then spent the night with the casket on the patio and other relatives stopped by with candles. There was no caravan to the cemetery, and the process of closure was complicated further by the inability to obtain a document certifying the death of the *abuelita*, reportedly thanks to some local scam involving falsified COVID death certificates and the wrath of insurance companies. The whole extended family meanwhile came down with the virus but survived, although it was a close call in the case of Tío Beto, who despite his dire state was refused admittance to the hospital. When a doctor somewhere was finally persuaded to assess Beto's condition, he declared that hospital admittance was a death sentence anyway and prescribed isolation at home.

Back in May, Javier and I took our own morbid dilemma to Horacio, a humble and garrulous restaurant proprietor from Mexico City who had resided in Zipolite for more than thirty years. His restaurant was located a few hundred meters back from the beach, behind but fortunately out of view of the yellow monstrosity of Canadian-inhabited condominiums, and to the side of the seemingly terminally ill mangrove. Though officially closed for *Quédate en casa*, Horacio let Javier and me set up our traveling mezcal-and-red-wine collection on one of his outdoor wooden tables and be devoured by mosquitoes while he busied himself smothering in garlic and then grilling whatever the fishermen of Puerto Ángel had caught that day. As soon as he ceased speaking for more than a split second, we asked him about *la playa de la muerte*.

Horacio was of the conviction that the name Zipolite was nothing more than a variation on *zopilote*, meaning vulture, of which there were many—and had apparently been even more during the heyday of the (now-shuttered) turtle slaughterhouse in the nearby village of San Agustinillo. This, however, did not stop him from embarking on a forty-five-minute review of all the *muertes* he himself had witnessed over the years. There was that one Semana Santa when he swore he counted eight deaths on one-third of the beach alone, leading him to calculate that there must have been upwards of twenty in total. Then there was the Christmas Eve when the niece of so-and-so announced she was going to change into her angel costume for the Nativity play and promptly died. ("That gave me the chills," said Horacio, rubbing his arms.) And the newlyweds on their final day of honeymoon in Zipolite who went to bid the sea farewell and drowned instead.

Following the tally of *muertes*, Horacio undertook to recreate the scream emitted by people being swept away by the current, which, he said, could be heard all the way from his restaurant. Upon noticing the state of petrified catatonia into which I had entered, he waved his hand and said this was all before the deployment of a smattering of lifeguards on the beach—at least during non-corona periods—who were capable of rescuing folks even while stoned. Javier was then permitted to contribute a memory, from once upon a time, of being swept out to sea naked on the Roca Blanca side of the beach and treading water for three hours before being deposited on Playa del Amor and making the trek back for his shorts. This was before nudity had been legalized in Zipolite, Javier said, when the military would beat apprehended nudists and/or make them perform push-ups. Memory completed, Horacio and Javier moved on to reminiscing about earthquakes and hurricanes that had struck the area.

And so the days passed on the beach of love and death. Sporadic rains came, things turned green, and a sudden proliferation of yellow butterflies fueled suspicion that we were actually living in Macondo. Javier made strides in conquering the internet, and added listening to Bach on his cell phone to the seaside regimen of smoking and writing in his notebook. Filling one notebook, he started on the next. I never asked for precise details of the content, but sometimes he would peruse his output from months before and, with a satisfied shake of the head, pronounce: *"Pinche Javier."* On occasion, I would bring my own notebook and write, as well, only to be repeatedly reminded that writing in the dark while partaking of wine had only aggravating effects on my already illegible script.

For the first few months of our coronavirus coexistence, Javier and I maintained a nontechnological rapport, owing to my lack of a phone and Javier's inability to remember his email address. This meant that, whenever I wanted to see him, I would just show up to the beach, or to his plot of land on the hill, or to his auto parts shop, where he also slept at night in a back room on a woven *petate* on the floor. But when the elusiveness of the Wi-Fi at my apartment rendered it categorically impossible to accomplish any work, I was forced to equip myself with a SIM card. After several days of mental preparation for the event, I was escorted by Javier on his motorbike to Puerto Ángel and the Oxxo convenience store, a ubiquitous component of Mexico's NAFTA-cultivated landscape. As a 2017 *New York Times* piece titled "A Nasty, NAFTA-Related Surprise: Mexico's Soaring Obesity," noted:

The top two grocery chains and most of the top food service outlets in Mexico are American backed or partners with companies like Walmart, Subway and Pizza Hut. Oxxo, the convenience store chain, is owned by Femsa, a Mexican food and beverage conglomerate that received hundreds of millions of dollars in foreign investment, helping it grow to 16,000 stores from 400 in 1990.

On the eve of NAFTA in 1993, the *Times* reported, Coca-Cola had paid $195 million for a third of Femsa's soft-drink unit. Walmart was now Mexico's largest food retailer, while Oxxo was second in grocery market share. (In 2010, the *Times'* Thomas Friedman had enthused about Walmart de México's scheduled opening that year of three hundred new stores, in an article in which he also cited a study of the top Mexican baby names, including Elizabeth, Karen, Kevin, and Bryan—in other words, "Not only Juans," which was apparently irrefutable proof of the correlation between free trade and societal advancement.) And while U.S. appetites had grown exponentially for avocados and other nutritious exports from warmer climes south of the border, Mexico had endured an influx of crap. As former Mexican dictator Porfirio Díaz, who perished in 1915, is said to have once lamented: "Poor Mexico, so far from God, so close to the United States." When Javier and I entered the Puerto Ángel Oxxo, then, we found ourselves surrounded by carbonated beverages, chips, hot dogs, and other neoliberal toxins—and face-to-face with a cashier woman who was openly horrified by our ignorance of the basics of modern telecommunications. Our questions ran along the lines of: "So, like, how do you put internet in the phone?"

The next step was for Javier and me to add each other on WhatsApp, which only happened thanks to the benevolent intervention of a neighbor in Zipolite and caused Javier to tsk at our incompetence: *"Qué pena, cabrón."* Javier was ahead of me on the WhatsApp front, having already mastered the sending of voice messages and GIFs, and he played a voice message for me from his seven-year-old grandson in Mexico City congratulating him on *finally* learning the GIF. Once Javier and I had been added to each other's contact lists, I found myself on the receiving end of GIFs in honor of "Hug Your Cat Day" and other occasions.

In the offline world, I was on the receiving end of a book by the name of *Hablan los Valientes de Zipolite*, by a certain Graciela Barabino, published in 2015. It was given to me by an old friend of Javier's, Carlos, whom Javier called Carlitos, and who with his wife presided over a couple of cabañas on the beach in front of which Javier always sat. The book purports to tell the history of the valiant 1970s struggle resulting in the recuperation of 73,898 hectares of communal land—in Zipolite and surrounding areas—that had ended up in the hands of wealthy caciques after being illegally expropriated by Víctor Bravo Ahuja, a former governor of Oaxaca. Post-governorship, Bravo Ahuja served as secretary of public education during the presidency of Luís Echeverría (1970–76), whose educational initiatives included the June 1971 *Halconazo* massacre of student protesters in Mexico City by state-sponsored, U.S.-trained paramilitaries (not to be confused with the 1968 Tlatelolco massacre of student protesters in Mexico City by the U.S.-backed state).

Incidentally, the land struggle in Zipolite also had an educational theme: it was touched off by the refusal of the caciques to part with even a spot of their precious, unused real estate such that the children of the village might have a school. After all, the plan was to sell the land to the federal government for tourism development without having to waste time dealing with the needs of the humans inhabiting the territory. In a rare stroke of misfortune for the superrich, however, it was discovered that Bravo Ahuja's expropriation of prime coastal land as well as inland areas was a direct violation of a 1953 decree by then-president of Mexico Adolfo Ruiz Cortines, establishing the communal nature of the land in question. Of course, the caciques didn't go down without a fight, and the military was dispatched to Zipolite to antagonize the community and hunt down a most-wanted list of particularly problematic characters, who promptly fled to the surrounding hills. But at the end of the day, in August 1979, the *zipoliteños* emerged victorious, and the land hoarders found themselves relieved of not merely a few square meters for a school but of 73,898 hectares—although some 12,000 of them would reportedly magically disappear into the Bahías de Huatulco tourism project.

Regrettably, *Hablan los Valientes* is often indistinguishable from a biography of Californian Gloria Hope Johnson—also referred to as Gloria Esperanza Johnson—who, we learn on page 267, was the very source of the idea for the manuscript, and who by her own account appears to have staged a Columbus-type discovery of Zipolite in 1969. In Mexico on holiday with two friends and thinking herself bound for Oaxaca's Puerto Escondido, Gloria instead wound up in Puerto Ángel, where, she says, "there was noth-ing"—which seems rather doubtful since Barabino has just written on the previous page that, from 1930–65, Puerto Ángel was "one of the most important ports in the Pacific." As Gloria recalls, the travelers' reception by the natives was less than welcoming, owing in part, she reckons, to her diamond nose ring—a "symbol and reminder of my spiritual mission in this life" but simultaneously a cause of public suspicion on account of her "gypsy appearance." Anyway, not much time was spent in Puerto Ángel, as Gloria & Co. set out walking on a dirt road and soon arrived at Gloria's Columbus moment in Zipolite: a "deserted beach," an "Eden!"—never mind the people living there—and a place where "divine energy emanated from every rock and bit of vegetation." This is where Gloria "belonged. Here and nowhere else." She had "discovered her cosmic path," and, as one does, she soon went about purchasing a hill at the far end of the beach (near the Roca Blanca pension where I stayed upon my own less momentous arrival in 2020). According to her, she was the only one who dared to live by the sea, as the other villagers feared reprisals by the cacique Manuel Galguera, who viewed the strip of sand as his personal lebensraum. In Barabino's tale, Gloria was the veritable "*corazón*" of the Zipolite land struggle, organizing the inhabitants of Eden so that all might live cosmically ever after. She continues to preside over a hillside spiritual retreat center here called, of course, Shambhala.

Presenting me with his copy of the book, Javier's friend Carlitos specified that, in lieu of returning it to him, I could simply burn it. A participant in the battle to regain the usurped hectarage, Carlitos was one of the twenty-eight villagers who had fled to the hills, where—when it became clear that the military weren't going to harm the villagers' families down below—the initial fear passed and a grand old time was evidently had over mezcal, smokable substances, and comradely conversation. Carlitos makes several appearances throughout the book, including with a rant about how Zipolite's striking victory was later betrayed when the *comuneros* started selling off the best lands and everything became about money. He also recounts a tragedy that "united us just as the land struggle did," when, one Sunday during the halftime of a soccer match, a rogue wave rose up from the otherwise placid water and swept away the swimming children. Carlitos and other *compañeros* took off in a *cayuco* and rescued them all—except for Daisy, who was swallowed by the sea and who, legend has it, now appears on occasion in Zipolite at night. Barabino takes this opportunity to remind us about *playa de la muerte*, and throws in some additional theories—beyond the "countless" drownings—as to the origins of the name. One of these is that, for the indigenous Zapotecs and Mixtecs, Zipolite's position at the southernmost point of Oaxacan territory rendered it "the end of the world, a kind of Mictlán" or underworld. A non-death-related suggestion is that the name Zipolite comes from "*Ce-pul-ithoa*," which Barabino says means "*lugar de gran visión*," or "place of great vision," in the Zapotec language.

C*e-pul-iThoa; Lugar de Gran Vision*" is also what's painted on a wall abutting the sand beneath the Shambhala hillside complex in Zipolite—although you'll only see it if you've decided to sit or engage in some other activity under a wooden porch that juts out over the wall, obscuring the painted sign that additionally proclaims, in Spanish: "Where man is one with nature . . . and nature is one with man." Beneath this, the word "Namaste" appears in quotation marks.

I discovered the sign when I hid under the porch in question for no fewer than six hours one day, equipped with a Tupperware of ceviche and a bottle of wine, in an effort to socially distance to the maximum extent possible from the checkpoint in front of my house. In those six hours, I was interrupted only by a darting iguana and a blonde woman crab-walking naked down the beach. My need for *sana distancia* had been made all the more acute with the upgrading of the checkpoint mix to encompass the Mexican Marines, whose penchant for stationing themselves and their armaments directly next to my front door made me jump out of my skin every time I opened it. Sometimes, a camouflage vehicle with a turret-like accessory was also parked on the grass in front of the door. The Marines were not much for conversation, but an uncharacteristically chatty one cornered me while I was trying to escape to the sea, and, finding out my national origin, launched into a friendly monologue on how there are too many rules in *Estados Unidos* and if you break them they treat you like an *animalito*. Here in Mexico, *gracias a dios*, we are free, he said. Other highlights of cohabitation with the checkpoint included the conversion of the space outside the window behind my bed into an open-air urinal, thanks to which it is possible that I have now seen more Mexican security forces pee than anyone in the world.

Fortuitously, the thermometer gun that made it into the hands of the checkpoint personnel was withdrawn the same day, and I no longer had to have my temperature taken every time I entered or exited the house.

The checkpoint operation had been given another one-month lease on life on May 30, when a meeting of the local assembly was held at the outdoor basketball court by the soccer field. The ostensible purpose of the event was for the *pueblo* to decide whether to dismantle the checkpoints and reopen the village to tourism. Although the economic ramifications of COVID-19 on the so-called Oaxacan Riviera were marginally buffered given that the virus struck as high season was winding down, the situation was obviously still dire. Earlier in May, the Mexican government agency CONEVAL had reported that up to 10.7 million Mexicans could be driven into extreme poverty in 2020 as a result of the pandemic. Javier had been eagerly awaiting the assembly meeting, relish as he did any good democratic spectacle, and had brought a small wooden stool on which to sit; the rest of us sat on the cement floor or stood. Face masks were few and far between. The master of ceremonies was assembly head Toño of the swimming lesson fetish, who began by declaring that, since we weren't even supposed to be having gatherings in times of coronavirus, this would have to be short. In the end, this meant two and a half hours.

As per Toño's calculations, were Zipolite to reopen its gates, there would be an immediate stampede from all over Mexico, because they had all been *encerrados* while we in Zipolite were *libres*. People want to come eat fish, Toño said. We've been at the checkpoint for sixty days, and every day we've eaten fish. It is important to eat fish and vegetables, he emphasized. After all insights had been exhausted, it was time for the *pueblo* to opine, and a line formed for the microphone. One villager argued that just because nobody had money didn't mean we should rush to invite corona-chaos into our midst; another proclaimed dramatically that he would prefer to die of hunger than to die of COVID. Others questioned the efficacy of the checkpoints since new faces kept popping up in Zipolite, while an older woman took to the stage with the uplifting reminder that we could also all be killed by dengue.

At some point, Toño entered conniption-fit mode and wrested the microphone back to inform the group that, contrary to his own pronouncements, the resumption of tourism was not even on the table, and we were merely talking about reopening taquerías. He was furthermore displeased that persons who did not own property insisted on coming to these meetings and trying to tell everyone what to do—to which someone else responded that the effects of the pandemic were not restricted to the property-owning class. Ultimately, it didn't matter who qualified as the real *pueblo* and who didn't, as the traditional end-of-meeting vote was discarded in favor of a decree from on high that the quarantine regime would stay largely as is, with the addition of tacos. Other minor adjustments were also made, and the checkpoint closing time was moved from 9 to 8 p.m. (after which the rope that stretched across the road by day was replaced with a medley of wire barricades, and the police played on their cell phones in the dark). Toño concluded the meeting with a menacingly upbeat "See you at the checkpoint!", and the crowd dispersed. Javier packed up his wooden stool, miffed about the contravention of democracy but professing *inmensa gratitud* for the chance to remain stuck in Zipolite.

On the day that I hid under the Shambhala porch for six hours, then, the complex was empty, which was one of the reasons I had chosen the spot; the other was that it was at exactly the opposite end of the beach from the freedom-loving Marines. I crawled under the porch with my Turkish Airlines blanket and ingestible goodies, took a deep breath, and attempted my own experiment in *inmensa gratitud*, encouraging my brain to view with favor my own sudden forcible immobility. In the very least, I reasoned, the indefinite pause in frenetic international movement spared me the self-imposed pressure to be omnipresent—to spend my life careening from place to place while sorting the minutiae of future travel itineraries and remembering where in the world I had left what rather than, you know, sitting under a porch. Things were decisively out of my control, and I should take advantage of the chance to purge the anal-retentive inner child, who used to make to-do lists like: "Brush teeth. Put on clothes. Play with dog 10 minutes. Play with Barbies 10 minutes. Do spelling homework."

Indeed, I told my brain, I had spent nearly two decades pursuing parallel lives in disparate geographies, leaving bits and pieces of me here and there and producing a scattered and incoherent sense of self. *Quédate en casa* was, therefore, an ideal moment to *un*-scatter: to sweat in place in Zipolite, watch ants crawl across my stomach, and focus on being one person for a change. By the end of the six hours and the bottle of wine, I had successfully alternated between fascination for my ostensible newfound capacity for stillness and tranquility and wanting to strangle myself for descending into triteness of *Eat, Pray, Love* proportions. (The "Namaste" did not help.) Auto-strangulation was, however, quickly averted when any semblance of serenity vanished in the first ten steps of my trek home, and my mind resumed lurching in deranged fashion between countries, people, trajectories, selves. It was like a high-speed word association game in which none of the memories were associated beyond the fact that they all belonged to me, and I fretted over what sort of catastrophic miswiring neurologists would find were they to inspect the interior of my head. In a matter of seconds, I would go from almonds in the Samarkand bazaar to clinging to the side of a rock over a precipice in Oman (where a friend had convinced me that "hiking" would be enjoyable) to a thermos in Vietnam to that time I simultaneously maintained five amorous relationships in as many countries to, finally, Uma. And all of this with a nagging passage from *Zorba the Greek* in my mental background:

You've seen, haven't you, Zorba, what happens when you place a magnifying glass in sunshine and gather its rays into just a single spot? The spot soon bursts into flames. Why? Because the sun's power is not dispersed but is entirely concentrated on that spot. The same happens with the human mind. You produce miracles if you cast your mind on one and only one thing. Do you understand, Zorba?

I met Uma in Sarajevo in 2016, when she was six years old and I was en route to Montenegro by bus. I briefly rented a small, damp apartment from her mom and dad, who had served as a paramedic and a militant, respectively, during the siege of the city in the 1990s. On this and my next several visits to Bosnia, Uma spoke little of the English language aside from the refrain to the Jennifer Lopez song "Ain't Your Mama," but we played games of hide-and-seek across from the bridge where Franz Ferdinand was assassinated in 1914—the catalyst for World War I—and held limbo tournaments and dance parties in her parents' living room, while they sat on the couch and chain-smoked. When I returned to Sarajevo in 2018, Uma had spontaneously acquired English and could now keep me apprised of my every faux pas, from wearing my ponytail wrong to pathologically mispronouncing *mjenjačnica* (exchange office) and *buregdžinica* (phyllo-dough pie shop) to incorrectly maneuvering the console for the Michael Jackson video dance game. Often, disapproval was registered via the deployment of her signature critique: "Not too genius." That winter, Uma and I would clock countless hours of said video dance game—Uma's favorite was "In the Closet," which she always won by a significant margin—when everything froze and it became impossible to go anywhere without sliding down a hill of ice to the street. A kind of quarantine in its own right, the Sarajevan winter experience was not conducive to miracle production in the least, as I spent much of my non–Michael Jackson time drinking *rakija* in the bathtub and reminiscing about the sun, which certainly wouldn't be piercing Bosnian magnifying glasses any time soon.

In Zipolite, on the other hand, it was impossible to escape the sun, yet I wasn't producing any miracles here, either—and I mean "miracles" in a relative, personal sense, i.e., writing work performed in a state of focused concentration rather than while mentally ricocheting between Bolivia, Lichtenstein, and Bulgaria. (On the bright side, the frenzied mental travel itinerary was at least a plus for the environment, as it was all happening in the confines of my head and did not require me to jet around as usual polluting the planet.) It was easy enough to *think* about writing and doing all sorts of things, but physically carrying these things out was an entirely different matter, and—while I did force myself to jog on a regular basis, this being my best defense against a total emotional meltdown—I would sometimes spend half a day in the hammock thinking about how I needed to squeeze a lime into my water, only to never do it. With Javier, too, I devoted an incredible amount of time making simple plans that never materialized, like eating carnitas on Sunday morning. We planned for me to learn to drive the motorbike and for Javier to catch a lobster—neither of which transpired even when the lobster plan was downgraded to simply finding a plastic cord to fish with. We planned to acquire a cow, which sounded like a gratifying undertaking. The cow was expensive. Javier continued to reiterate his plan for a better and more harmonious world to rise from the ashes of the pandemic and for the old world to *chingar a su madre*, but we made even less progress in that direction.

A sort of time warp took hold, I couldn't tell whether as a result of the quarantine or the essence of Zipolite or both. The time warp applied to the microlevel—extended contemplation of lime-squeezing, etc. —and the macro alike. When my parents emailed on day fifty of their Barcelona lockdown with the daily update on number of COVID deaths in Spain and number of times the apartment shelves had been polished, I couldn't fathom what I myself had been doing for fifty entire days of my own non-lockdown. (Things would get even more confounding come September, when my six-month Mexican visa would expire, and, while still having nothing to say for myself, I'd also be faced with the reality of having been in one fixed spot for longer than at any point since high school—with no concrete plans for onward movement.) The days, it seemed, passed at once too slowly and too fast, as though time somehow flies when you're zapping mosquitoes with an electric racket and watching policemen urinate outside your window. Whereas my former modus operandi had been to defy the law of inertia whenever possible, weird stuff was now happening, and I became increasingly resilient to even the most minor changes—when I had previously thrived on change and change alone. For example, for my first few months in Zipolite, a white van was parked next to the soccer field where I jogged, across from Javier's Autopartes El Sol. In the van slept a couple, of undetermined nationality, whose names I never knew but whose laundry I was intimately acquainted with, hanging as it was every morning from a rope tied to a tree. Javier once made them a target of his unsolicited mango delivery service, a kindness they repaid by gifting him a jar of marmalade, but he had no input on names or country of origin. Despite the fact that I had not interacted with the couple on a single occasion, I lost it when Javier informed me one evening that the van was gone. We were walking back from Horacio's along the beach when I received the news. Feeling as though my entire world had come crashing down around me, I stopped in my tracks and commenced whimpering about why and how and where did they go, while Javier took a drag on his cigarette and observed me with curiosity.

One activity Javier and I did manage to accomplish rather than simply sitting on our asses and talking about it forever was a bougainvillea-buying excursion to a nursery in the neighboring municipality of Santa María Tonameca, which was only made possible when the San Agustinillo and Mazunte checkpoints decided to start letting the Zipolite folk through and vice versa. There was a certain exhilarating sensation as we crossed into heretofore forbidden lands, even though I still had to present my coronavirus ID at every stop along with a compelling reason for needing to buy flowers. Traversing the checkpoints additionally required being repeatedly doused with disinfectant and gel, a process that became more interesting on the ride home, after Javier had added rose bushes to his shopping list and the motorbike had transformed into a mobile botanical garden-cum-shield-from-incoming-spray.

Another excursion that after much deliberation and delay finally came to fruition was a visit to Toño of Lo Cósmico, not to be confused with Toño of village assembly petulance. This Toño was a longtime pal of Javier's, a key participant in the Zipolite land struggle, and a former beau of Gloria's; Lo Cósmico was the name of his hillside cabañas, just a couple of stone's throws down the beach from Shambhala. Javier and I arrived unannounced one morning to the hotel, also shuttered for coronavirus, to find Toño on the patio at the top of the hill, clad in underwear and a cape-type garment and having seemingly consumed an extraordinary quantity of coffee. Concurring that the *nueva normalidad* and its social distancing protocol could *irse a la chingada*, Toño and Javier threw their arms around each other, after which greeting session Toño was forced to administer first aid to the minor wounds Javier and I had just sustained when Javier had sought to execute a high-speed turn on the motorbike in the mud. Ointments applied, we settled in on the patio to absorb Toño's stream of consciousness, interspersed with shouts of *"¡PIEDRAS NO!"*, directed at his large dog, who had learned to heave rocks at guests with his mouth.

Three hours later, Toño had time-traveled from the coronavirus to Benito Juárez and back—with stops along the way including the solar eclipse of March 7, 1970, the Mexican Revolution and land reform, and the privatization binge overseen by U.S. acolyte Carlos Salinas de Gortari, president of Mexico from 1988–94 and co-father of NAFTA, who had found most arousing the idea of offering up communally owned lands for corporate plunder. Apologizing for his longwinded route, Toño explained that the problem was there was so much history that one didn't know where to begin or to end, and told me I could go lie in the hammock if I needed a break from him. Javier's participation in the verbal extravaganza consisted of recalling mutual acquaintances who had died and singing, with Toño, an old song called "Zipolite Beach," written by people who had also died.

Like Javier, Toño had first come into contact with Zipolite during the so-called "eclipse of the century," which had put the village on the cosmic map, as it were. The epicenter of the total eclipse was Miahuatlán, Oaxaca, several hours to the north, where international scientists had descended in honor of the phenomenon—meriting the following anthropological investigation by *The New York Times*' Walter Sullivan, who apparently forgot what century he was reporting from:

> There are few regions of the Americas where the inhabitants are less acquainted with the ways of

science than this one . . . Yet the inhabitants are insatiably curious. The astronomers complain, not about thievery or hostility, but about being constantly on stage, so to speak. Clusters of the broad-faced Zapotecs stand and watch, grinning, from dawn to dusk as the teams prepare and rehearse for the crucial minutes of eclipse.

For Javier, the eclipse-viewing expedition was a natural step on the path to reorienting his life around drug use rather than a professional soccer career. Toño, on the other hand, was a student in Mexico City at the time, and had volunteered to help transport telescopes and other equipment to Oaxaca, where a scientific encampment would also be set up in Zipolite. "Can you believe it took thirty-six hours—*¡PIEDRAS NO!*—to get here from the capital," Toño remarked, leaping up from his chair to fling a sandal down the hillside, momentarily distracting the dog from his rock-heaving mission. I brought up Graciela Barabino's *Hablan los Valientes de Zipolite*, in which she gushes about how "Toño never imagined that the eclipse would change his life forever, introducing him to a world that was real, wild, and fascinating, where the true authority is wielded by nature, in divine democracy." (Somehow, Zipolite also instantaneously cured him of chronic migraines and intolerance to sunlight.) Pausing just long enough to remind himself that he'd been meaning to sue Barabino for reproducing his news archives and documents without proper credit, he resumed his tumbling narrative with a recap of Juárez's belief in the separation of church and state.

In post-eclipse Mexico City, Toño had worked as a librarian at the National Institute of Nuclear Energy before going on to serve as a leader in the electrical workers' union, a choice that promptly caused him to fear for his life. He fled to Zipolite in the mid-seventies with, he said, enough money to survive for one and a half months at the house of Tía Susana, whom he had met during the eclipse and whom he defined as the *"eje matriarcal"*—the matriarchal axis—of the village. In the early days, she was the only villager with a shop (and a Chevy truck named Marisol), and her home was a landmark for residents of Zipolite and visitors alike. I had already heard innumerable stories about her from Javier, who called her Doña Susanita and placed her at the very top of the list of the many honorary *madres* he'd had in Zipolite. The list also featured Doña Susanita's own mother, Tía Máxima—who used to let Javier grind coffee for a peso, which, he specified, was worth much more before Salinas de Gortari *nos chingó*—and Tía Rafaelita, who despite her own precarious economic situation made sure that all his papaya and banana needs were met.

When Toño arrived back to Zipolite mid-decade, Doña Susanita gave him a space to sleep and two meals a day. And it was with Doña Susanita that he would soon approach the cacique Manuel Galguera to request a bit of land to build a school for the children of the village. Gesturing at the wide table in front of him on the patio, Toño jabbed his finger on a tiny speck in one corner: This is what we were asking for, and we even offered to pay for it. Galguera couldn't be bothered, so off went the ex-librarian to unearth the 1953 presidential decree establishing the land as communal. In the ensuing struggle, Toño would hide out in the hills with Carlitos and the other villagers and complete a brief but abusive stint in jail, from which he was bailed out by Doña Susanita, who fashioned a short-term solution for his newly fractured vertebrae using an orange crate and cloth. A midwife and de facto village doctor specializing in injections and herbal treatments, Doña Susanita's expertise expanded, Toño said, when he presented her with a giant medical book following the traumatic death of an ill child who had been unable to reach Pochutla in time. We were just about to plunge back into the Mexican Revolution when Toño received a phone call from someone requiring extensive animated counsel, which the dog interpreted as the opportunity of a lifetime. Javier and I prepared our exit strategy.

Prior to her death in 1994, Doña Susanita had rescued Javier from many a mishap, earning herself the most *inmensa* of gratitudes and the title of *madre protectora*. There was the time he fell off the roof in the middle of the night and royally battered his head, a not insignificant event on the Zipolite timeline, as it turned out. When Javier and I visited a neighbor who ran a *temazcal*—a pre-Hispanic sweat lodge packaged, in this case, for the spiritually inspired capitalist and other international consumers of cultural caricature—she remembered him as "the guy who fell off Tía Susana's roof forty years ago." Then there was the time he was stung by a scorpion while tripping on mushrooms in the forest, for which Doña Susanita prescribed a treatment of limes. And then there was the bout of malaria, which required cinchona bark and other materials as well as forcible internment in Doña Susanita's home until the illness had run its course. When Javier's real mother and grandmother visited him in Zipolite shortly after the roof incident, he was pleased that all of his *madres* got along.

I meanwhile found myself wishing for my very own Doña Susanita when I spent an entire night being violently ill in the bathroom—a result of reckless horizontal overconsumption of tamales and mezcal on the beach—with an audience of Marines outside my window. I wished the same when I sustained three consecutive wasp stings to the ankle on the soccer field, rendering me immobile and whiny for a varying number of days each time, and again when a 7.4 magnitude earthquake rocked Oaxaca on June 23, followed by a tsunami warning in Zipolite and elsewhere along the coast. Not long after that, I came down with typhoid, which I had wrongly believed to have been eradicated centuries ago. This left me ever more convinced that *playa de la muerte* was a foregone conclusion, and that I was simply going through the motions.

The night before he was stricken with malaria, Javier had a dream about a tsunami. In it, he was standing on a pier as the wave approached. He began to run, and, in the course of his flight, found a girl buying fruit from an old woman. He yelled at the girl to join him, because the sea "*nos va a llevar a la chingada.*" They took off, hand in hand, for the mountains, whereupon they came across a church, which, despite its huge appearance, was actually very small. The girl tried to drag him inside. He resisted, but she was adamant: "No, *cabrón*, it will save us." She smiled *una sonrisa loca*, and Javier woke up.

The next morning, Javier set out by donkey for Puerto Ángel, where he would leave the donkey and continue by truck to Pochutla to complete errands for Doña Susanita. On the way, he passed a hut where he saw—"*no mames*"—the very same girl with the very same smile. He made it to Pochutla and back before delirium struck and Doña Susanita took over, and he never saw the girl with the smile again, either in dreams or reality. She would certainly stage an appearance in my own mind, however, when, shortly after 10:30 a.m.

on June 23, a car came speeding through the check-point in front of my apartment with assorted passengers hanging out the windows, screaming at everyone to run for the hills or else face death-by-tsunami.

At 10:29, I had been settling into my chair in the corner for some article-writing, congratulating myself on having resisted the temptation to have wine for breakfast—a clear sign I was getting my life in order. Then, suddenly, I was bolting across the room for the door, which is evidently the instinctive human reaction when your immediate environment shudders in a man-ner that suggests impending self-combustion. Outside, the power lines were sparking every which way, the checkpoint personnel were in disarray, and I sought a position of relative safety in the middle of the street, where I was able to beleaguer the multitude with perti-nent questions like: "What is happening?" and "Will it stop?" Entering a state of semi-suspended animation, I recalled Horacio's firsthand account of the Mexico City earthquake of 1985, and how he'd said that, while he had been accustomed to seeing corpses, he had not been accustomed to seeing them flattened like tortillas. The electrical sparks subsided, and a general consensus was reached that my house would not collapse on top of me if I went back inside it, which I did, only to be jolted back out by the tsunami-mobile. As the police mounted their vehicles and everyone else made a break for it, I played the role of Gringa in Doorway Having Flashbacks to TV Coverage of Indian Ocean Tsunami of 2004.

One of the checkpoint regulars, a large man who looked to be in his fifties and who brought his own reflective vest to checkpoint duty, made eye contact with me as he bounded toward his pickup truck, motioning for me to jump in: "We have to get to higher ground." I assumed he meant at least to the hilltop cemetery, which, in addition to being an apt point from which to view the potential death of *la playa de la muerte* down below, was where the *zipoliteños* had congregated during the last major earthquake and tsunami alert in 2017. This quake, which had been magnitude 8.2 and had struck off the coast of Chiapas, had also ultimately served Javier's vision of a more wholesome world. On various occasions, he had recalled with admiration the cooperative spirit he had witnessed that day around the cemetery—but, I had noticed, the admiration of an outsider looking in, whose function was to observe rather than participate in solidarity.

This time around, the cemetery was not our destination, and the pickup truck made it no farther than a few hundred meters up the road, where the man with the reflective vest resided with his extended family on a plot of land with numerous huts, hammocks, dogs, pigs, and chickens. As it had started to rain, I was ushered onto one of the patios, where much of the family was gathered. The grandfather chortled that surely my sheer terror was nothing a few shots of mezcal couldn't take care of, and thrust his cell phone screen in my direction such that his video-chat interlocutors—relatives abroad who were conducting the requisite post-seismic assessment—could see "what the earthquake brought us."

Other members of the family were comparing where-were-you-at-10:29 stories, with the prize for most entertaining going to the woman who had been sweeping the roof. I attempted to politely redirect the conversation onto the tsunami issue but was assured that the hill abutting the back of the property was more than fifteen meters high, allegedly making it almost 100 percent tsunami-proof—and that anyway José, another family member, was at the beach monitoring the sea level and would advise immediately if we had to evacuate for real.

I made small talk with the children, who, teary-eyed and with chins resting glumly on the table, were nonetheless somewhat intrigued by the presence of an adult who did not remotely have it together. While the rest of the family laughed and joked at each aftershock, I grimaced and dug my fingernails deeper into the skin on my thighs. A teenage girl put her hand on my shoulder and told me that, not to worry, I'd survive and go on to have children of my own if I weren't already too old; others from the group patiently responded to my repeated inquiries about how long the aftershocks would persist, whether there would be any particularly formidable ones, and so forth: "Only god knows." Others were preoccupied with the matter of "George," who, I soon realized, was George Floyd, the unarmed forty-six-year-old black man killed by Minneapolis cops on May 25— or, if you prefer the more sanitized media version, the latest black American to up and die in police custody through no fault of the individual officers or institutionalized racism. Ongoing protests against the slaying had provided the media watchdog group Fairness & Accuracy In Reporting with material for a compilation of the "Top 16 Euphemisms US Headline Writers Used for Police Beating the Shit Out of People," such as the *Washington Post*'s "Police Turn More Aggressive Against Protesters and Bystanders Alike, Adding to Disorder." The woman who had been sweeping the roof at 10:29 told me that, when she and her immediate family had done their own stint in the U.S. some years back, they had chosen Ohio as their destination based on a rumor they'd heard that it was less racist there. Empirical research, she said, had revealed this not to be the case.

One of the rooms off of the patio contained a television set that was partially visible through a window slat, offering glimpses of earthquake coverage in Huatulco, near where the epicenter had been, and Mexico City, which had also received a good shaking. (The intersection of seismic activity and pandemic had produced a conundrum, as news viewers in the Mexican capital were being told to evacuate their buildings while the *Quédate en casa* icon remained fixed on their screens.) I thought back to an earthquake I'd experienced in southern Turkey in 2011—where the principal peril had been not a tsunami but a wardrobe falling on my head—and to a Beirut car bomb in 2013, which I had initially misdiagnosed as either an earthquake or some sort of crazy hangover effect. I thought of the 2012 earthquake that had rattled me from my sleep in the Peruvian city of Ayacucho, birthplace of Sendero Luminoso, and of the *ayacuchano* who had sworn to me that, when the organization launched guerrilla warfare in the region in 1980, there had been earthquakes every five minutes. And I thought of the perennial tremors of the earth in San Salvador, which seemed like both just the other day and a lifetime ago.

José of sea-monitoring duties made several appearances to report that, while the water level in Zipolite was slightly altered, it was so far so good, and the patio gradually cleared out as mundane tasks resumed. The grandmother of the family—a robust woman named Susana in a red blouse, shorts, and flip-flops—moved to a chair next to mine and took one of the somber male children between her knees. For hours on end, I remained glued to my chair, unable to think of moving, even when José returned with the announcement that the coast, literally, was clear. Despite being once again tempted to bash my own head in and thereby put a stop to *Eat, Pray, Love*-style vapidity, I couldn't help but feel that this red-bloused woman emanated some sort of protective aura, and that I needed to sit in her shadow forever. Distinctly amused by the spectacle of me, Susana told me I was welcome to stay the night, or as long as I wanted, because the worst thing in times like these was to be *solita*. Eventually, I came to grips with the fact that it was only civilized to allow the family a respite from my presence, and dragged myself home to find the checkpoint empty, without even a single police-man in sight.

Feelings of abandonment and betrayal set in (and who was going to ensure that my face mask was in place?!). Pacing cautiously in my apartment so as not to disturb the tectonic plates, I alternated between peer-ing out the window and compulsively flinging open the front door to see if there was any sign of checkpoint repopulation. A few times, I crept out into the road, but experienced no joy in not having to step over the rope. The overcast sky and Doritos wrappers blowing down the street only added to the air of melancholy, and I sought refuge from the silence by recalling the high-lights of the past one and a half months: the coronavirus cumbia, the defecation on my doorstep, the joint civilian-police effort to exterminate the wasp that had taken up residence in my underwear drawer, the time I tattled with righteous indignation on some fellow gringos who had spontaneously surfaced in Zipolite despite the quarantine. (The police had responded with a shrug: "We know.") In my kitchen, I blasted eighties comfort music from my computer and cooked fish, without the typical running commentary from the checkpoint outside about the *novio* for whom I was allegedly cooking. When the whole scene had become too twilight zone to handle, I headed back up the road to clan Susana with a bottle of mezcal.

The family's base of operations had now relocated to a different patio with a hammock and large mattress, occupied by Susana and her husband Andrés, respectively. Andrés's belly hosted a rotation of grandchildren, who, having overcome the morning's scare, piled on top of him. Silence was intermittently called for as plot twists took place in the telenovela playing on the

TV set in between hammock and mattress, and I was reminded that I still had an hour and a half to go in the latest episode of my current Turkish telenovela—a doubly cathartic viewing exercise in that I got to cry not only in tandem with the characters but also out of nostalgia for Turkish landscapes and Turkish teapots and ever-gratifying Turkish expressions of frustration. Andrés welcomed the addition of mezcal to the present milieu, and the teenager who had put her hand on my shoulder set about grilling quesadillas. Susana reacted to some or other onscreen transgression, and reiterated the invitation for me to stay the night.

When I asked whether the couple had participated in the land struggle of the seventies, Susana responded with matter-of-fact irony that she had not since she was a woman. Andrés, who had participated, was of the opinion that it had been no big deal and was just your typical recuperation of 73,898 hectares. As Susana fielded a phone call, I asked Andrés if they had known Doña Susanita. He nodded at Susana: "She's her daughter."

The rest of the evening would see me traipse home, only to be carted back once again in the pickup truck by the relative in the reflective vest. He had been dispatched to fetch me on the orders of Susana, who had correctly predicted collateral psychological damage from the 5.5 magnitude aftershock that struck at 9:33 p.m. I was accommodated in a room that was adjacent to the patio where the entire family would be sleeping, in hammocks and tents, as per post-earthquake tradition. In the morning, following a night of aftershock-punctuated naps, I sat on the bed and watched through the window as the plot of land came to life—with things being wheelbarrowed around, animals being fed, and everything sweepable being swept: patio, street, dirt. Emmanuel Iduma's lines in *A Stranger's Pose*, about the Mauritanian men ambling home from the mosque, once again came to mind: "I envy the ardor in their gait, a lack of hurry, as if by walking they possess a piece of the earth . . . . I want to be these men." In the same book, Iduma writes: "A corpse is the foremost expression of sedentary life." But for a moment on that Zipolite morning, all I wanted was for the earth to be still beneath me.

Javier was temporarily irked that I had not come to the beach the night of the earthquake and tsunami warning, although he got over it when he found out I had been in the company of the daughter of Doña Susanita. Actually, he calculated, he had been one of only approximately two people on the beach that night, the other one a young man from Mexico City who had recently slipped through the checkpoint into Zipolite. His father had died of coronavirus, and he had come to the sea to grieve in a less oppressive setting. "First he sat behind me," Javier reported, "and I told him: 'What *chingados* are you doing, sitting behind someone in the dark?'" The young man had then sat next to him, and, while Javier had not been in the mood to talk, he had reckoned the social interaction would be mutually beneficial. By the end of it all, he was immensely grateful for the man's presence, and had even tried to share his mezcal: "I forgot about the *pinche* pandemic."

On June 25, two days after the earthquake and two days prior to the scheduled village assembly vote on the matter, the checkpoint in front of my apartment was dismantled. I wandered out the door to find the non–Lo Cósmico Toño loading tarps, water barrels, and other checkpoint accoutrements into the back of a truck. The unilateral dismantling decision had been made, Toño claimed, in order to facilitate vehicular escape in the event of another natural disaster. A policeman loitering under a tree suggested that this was a spectacular opportunity to crack open the beers; another recommenced telling me about that time in 2010 when he had worked at a restaurant in South Carolina, the one by the Walmart and the bridge (did I know it?). I barely heard any of them, though. I was too busy missing Zipolite— and I was still there.

EPILOGUE

In his 1688 dissertation at the University of Basel, Swiss medical student Johannes Hofer coined the term "nostalgia," a combination of the Greek *nostos*—meaning homecoming or return—and *algos*, meaning pain. An article in *The Atlantic* specifies that, for centuries, nostalgia was considered to be a "psychopathological disorder," necessitating prescribed treatments including "leeches, purging the stomach, and 'warm hypnotic emulsions.'" During the American Civil War, there were soldiers who literally died of nostalgia.

In my own case, a painful longing for the past has pretty much been my baseline mood since childhood. In later years, the condition was perhaps rendered increasingly eligible for psychopathological diagnosis by the fact that the desire for return was not limited to a single place but rather a bazillion different ones, none of them technically qualifying as "home." And in quarantined Zipolite, things became even more complicated with the onset of coronastalgia, if you will, which comprised anguished nostalgia for not only all of the things I already missed and the places I now couldn't go but also for the present quarantined moment and, if possible, nostalgia itself.

The physical inertia of the new arrangement endured well beyond the reopening of the checkpoints, and the refusal of time to halt in solidarity meant that it was soon September 5, 2020, which was one day prior to the expiration of my six-month Mexican visa and the day I had committed to flying from nearby Huatulco to Istanbul via Mexico City and Frankfurt. At the last minute, I couldn't bring myself to leave, and reasoned that it was futile to attempt to reinsert myself into civilization anyway, covered as I was in a seemingly permanent layer of sand. I was subsequently assured by a veteran visa-overstayer from Argentina in Zipolite that I could DHL my passport from Pochutla to a certain official in the Mexican capital, who for a modest fee would emblazon my document with a new, fake entry stamp. This, to be sure, was almost as formidable a hassle as those faced by Mexican and other asylum seekers in my own country, such as being put in cages and later deported. At any rate, I settled in for the indefinite future—stillness rather than frenetic motion having been deemed the preferred form of escape from a reality now defined by a pandemic.

And so it was that, when the iconic *Día de Muertos* commenced in Mexico on November 1, I found myself at the hilltop cemetery in Zipolite, eating a cookie next to the grave of Antonio I. Ruiz Altamirano in between overreacting to every Day of the Dead fireworks explosion set off in the vicinity. Javier was gone, having been forcibly diagnosed with homesickness by his family and repatriated to the state of Morelos in August, where he continued to send me seedling emojis on WhatsApp.

His replacement in the realm of requisite human social interaction was a 55-year-old doctor from Chiapas named Enrique, who had moved to Zipolite from the city of Tuxtla Gutiérrez in March, just three days after my own arrival. Motives for the move ranged from the pursuit of a simplified way of life in a seaside locale where clothing was not obligatory to the pursuit of a diet not based on Domino's Pizza and other American fast food staples. I had met Enrique on the beach one evening, when I sought his medical opinion on the local coronavirus response and was cheerfully informed that, if I absolutely had to contract the virus, it would be best to do so when there were available hospital beds in Oaxaca City seven hours away. He had charitably tended to me during my bout with typhoid, which alternately had me experiencing auditory hallucinations of mariachi music and reenacting the head-spinning scene from *The Exorcist*.

By the time the *Día de Muertos* rolled around, Enrique had shed more than twenty kilos, and he accompanied me on the morning trek up the hill to the diminutive cemetery with its giant painted Catrina skeleton at the entrance. A smattering of people was there paying respects to deceased loved ones, and most of the graves had already been inundated with the *cempazúchitl* flower—or Mexican marigold—along with candles and other ornaments. At the center of the cemetery, an overturned red plastic Coca-Cola crate added to the morbid aesthetics. We selected Antonio I. Ruiz Altamirano on account of the bench next to his grave, where we sat to rest and contemplate his lifespan: 1932–2002. He had entered the world during the presidency of Abelardo Rodríguez, founder of Petromex—the precursor of Pemex—and the Federal Electricity Commission, on whose watch were also laid the foundations of Mexico's short-lived "socialist education" program. He had exited the world during the reign of Vicente Fox, former Coca-Cola Mexico CEO and source of the idea that Mexican immigrants to the United States do jobs that "not even blacks want to do."

Recalling the Days of the Dead of his own childhood in Tuxtla, Enrique described the noisemaking devices he and his companions would fashion by placing rocks in beer cans—"It wasn't difficult to find those since our dads were all alcoholics"—with which they would then make rounds of the houses in the neighborhood in search of *calabacita*, a traditional pumpkin sweet. "At each house we would chant: 'We are *angelitos* who came down from heaven asking for *calabacita*.' Then we would pause. Then we would appeal to the lady of the house: '*Calabacita tía!*' If we got the *calabacita* we shouted '*Qué viva la tía!*'—or *el tío*, as the case sometimes was. If not we shouted '*Qué muera la tía!*'—or *el tío*—and took off running."

As a child, Enrique had shared a bedroom with his *abuelita* and sometimes a bed, usually on occasions when he was overcome with existential angst about what lay beyond the last star visible from the bedroom window. Further uncertainties involving space had arisen with the Apollo 13 episode in April 1970, a month after the solar eclipse, and his *abuelita* had taken him to church to pray for the crew. In one corner of the bedroom she maintained a permanent altar with carnations, basil, images of saints, and a figure of Jesus who was dressed, undressed, attached to a cross, and taken down accordingly. Each year on the Day of the Dead—as well as on late family members' birthdays and the anniversaries of their deaths—the altar expanded to include photos of the deceased, *aguardiente*, tamales, *calabacita*, and *cempazúchitl*. At night, Enrique recalled, the flowers were relocated to the patio due to a prevailing superstition concerning carbon dioxide emissions.

Now, half a century later, *Día de Muertos* festivities had been thrown off by coronavirus, and, instead of playing host to all-night gatherings with mariachis and refreshments, many Mexican cemeteries were simply dead. Graveyard closures and a ban on selling flowers at markets in certain cities was bad news indeed for flower farmers whose very livelihoods depended in good part on the Day of the Dead. AMLO had declared three days of national mourning, starting on October 31, for the victims of COVID-19, but the Army's attempts to put the giant flag in Mexico City's Zócalo at half-mast had been thwarted by protesters from FRENA, the National Anti-AMLO Front, who had been camped out since September in the plaza in a bid to save the country from alleged communist tyranny. In the Palacio Nacional, AMLO attended a ceremony featuring twenty altars installed by different indigenous groups, during which, Mexico's *La Jornada* newspaper specified, "neither the president nor his wife wore face masks, in contrast to the indigenous."

Enrique firmly believed that AMLO's opposition to neoliberal pillage made him hands down the best thing to happen to Mexico since Benito Juárez, and despite his employment in the medical field he had ceased following domestic coronavirus news; he had, however, verified that no virus tests existed anywhere in Pochutla or environs. Not long after the *Día de Muertos*, Mexico would become the fourth country in the

world to officially surpass 100,000 COVID deaths—
although the actual number was likely astronomically
higher—causing #DoctorMuerte to trend once again
on Twitter in reference to Mexican coronavirus czar
Hugo López-Gatell.

In Zipolite, the illusion of a protective coronavirus shield persisted notwithstanding the reopening
of the village to tourism, and rumors of cases were
generally but not always limited to Pochutla, Puerto
Ángel, and Mazunte. Back in August, Enrique had
been accosted by a distraught coconut vendor, who
had announced the coronavirus deaths of an elderly
brother and sister in Zipolite; the next day, the
brother and sister in question had materialized, alive,
on the beach, while a pair of siblings who had in fact
perished turned out to have done so thanks to something other than coronavirus. By November, there
were increasing reports that the virus had penetrated
the village. Also in circulation was a suggested virus
remedy that entailed binging on paracetamol while

soaking one's feet in a concoction made from leaves of the *cacahuanane* tree.

Enrique and I bade farewell to Antonio I. Ruiz Altamirano and headed back down the hill. I returned to my home, where the front yard had in the post-checkpoint era of *la nueva normalidad* become a frequent stopping point for the red truck that made daily rounds selling oranges. A loudspeaker attached to the vehicle exhorted all *señoras* and housewives within earshot to "come get your oranges"—even to "*demand* your oranges," as though they were some sort of endangered human right. (According to Enrique, the orange-selling truck in Tuxtla took a slightly different approach, which was to exhort the *señoras* to send their husbands out for the fruit.) I handed over thirty pesos—approximately a dollar and a half—to the assistant to the truck driver, and twenty-five oranges were shoveled into my bag. I went inside.

As of 5:30 p.m. on November 1, 2020, the National Seismological Service at the UNAM—the National

Autonomous University of Mexico—had registered no fewer than 13,527 aftershocks from the June 23 earthquake in Oaxaca. I never did figure out why I hadn't departed Zipolite in September as scheduled, and whether it was a result of acquired dependency on place of confinement or maybe had something to do with that old saying that "to leave is to die a little." But in the meantime, at least, it seemed plenty of movement was possible while standing still.

Belén Fernández is a contributing editor at *Jacobin*, and has written for *The New York Times*, the *London Review of Books* blog, *Current Affairs, Al Jazeera*, and *Middle East Eye*, among other outlets. She is the author of *Exile: Rejecting America and Finding the World* (OR Books, 2019), *Martyrs Never Die: Travels through South Lebanon* (Warscapes, 2016), and *The Imperial Messenger: Thomas Friedman at Work* (Verso, 2011).

Printed in the USA
CPSIA information can be obtained
at www.ICGtesting.com
JSHW082353140824
68134JS00020B/2051